The F*@#ing Wedding Calligraphy Workbook

By

Life Style Daily

Table of Contents:

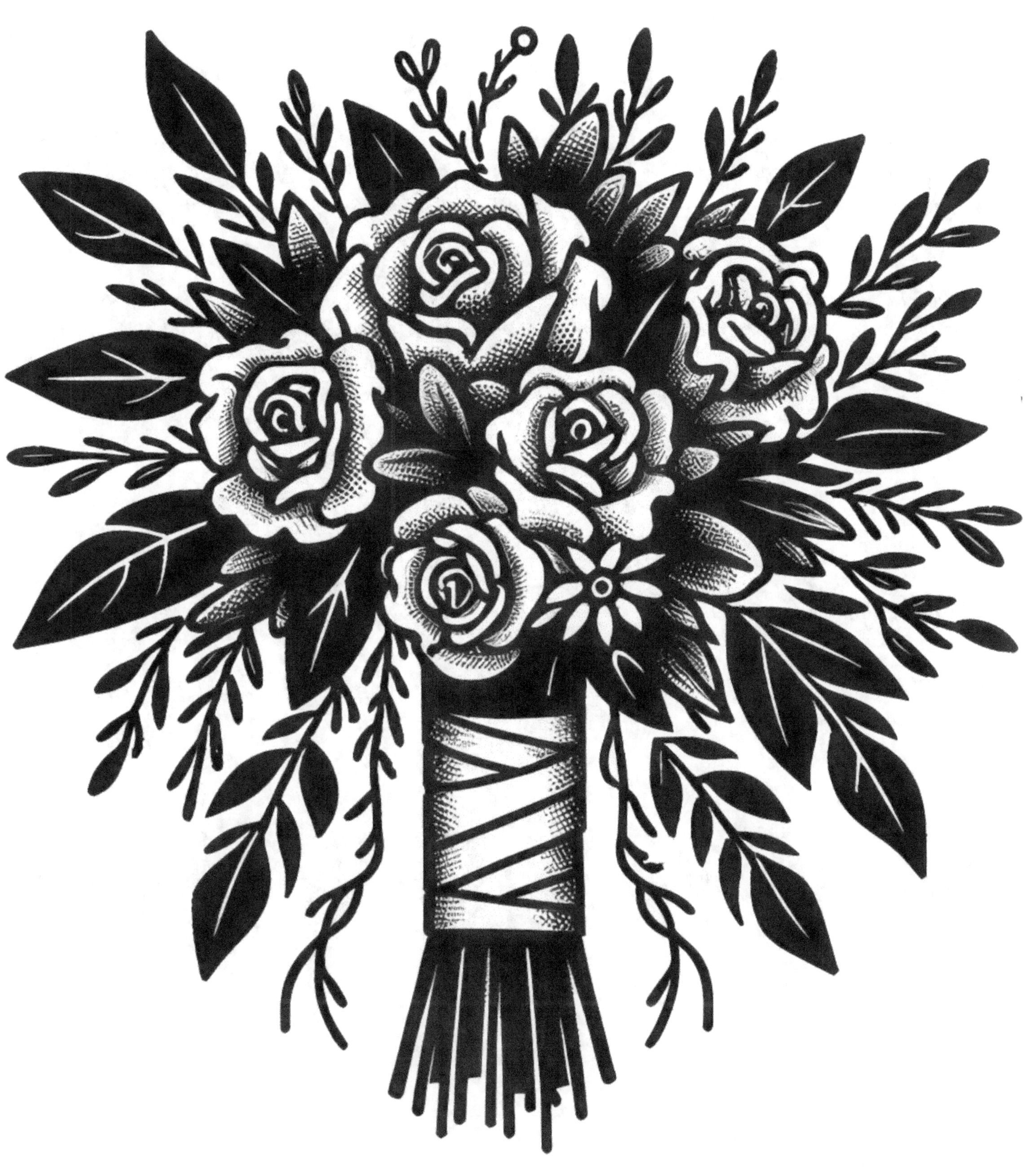

Chapter 1: The ABCs of Fucking Calligraphy

Section 11: Swearing 101: Your Crash Course in Vulgar Vocabulary

Welcome to Swearing 101, where we'll embark on a no-holds-barred journey into the art of colorful language. Whether you're a seasoned cusser or a budding profanity aficionado, this crash course will ensure your vocabulary is up to snuff for your Fucking Calligraphy adventures.

No discussion of classic expletives would be complete without the iconic F-word. It's versatile, impactful, and, when expertly placed in your calligraphy, can evoke laughter, shock, or sheer admiration. We'll delve into the many shades of "fuck," from its forceful presence to its subtle nuances.

The Almighty F-Word:

In Calligraphy: "This Fucking Love Is Eternal" - Perfect for a bold and unconventional wedding invitation.

Daily Life: Use sparingly in casual conversations for emphasis, but avoid in formal or professional settings.

This Fucking Love Is Eternal

This Fucking Love Is Eternal

This Fucking Love Is Eternal

"Fucking Finally! Join Us for Our Big Day."

Fucking Finally!
Join Us for Our Big Day

Mark Your Fucking Calendar Our Wedding Is Coming!

"Girls' Night Out: Let's Get Fucking Wild!"

Girls' Night Out
Let's Get Fucking Wild!

Girls' Night Out

Let's Get Fucking Wild!

Girls' Night Out

Let's Get Fucking Wild!

"Dance Floor Open: Get Ready to Fucking Party!"

Dance Floor Open
Get Ready to Fucking Party!

"Your Fucking Presence Meant the World to Us."

Your Fucking Presence Meant the World to Us

The All-Purpose S-Word: "Shit" is another staple of profanity. Its adaptability is unmatched—it can serve as a noun, verb, adjective, or interjection, depending on the context. We'll explore the various ways to employ this versatile word in your calligraphy to convey your message with a dash of irreverence

The All-Purpose S-Word:

In Calligraphy: "Shit Just Got Real" - Ideal for a humorous save-the-date card.

Daily Life: Use to express surprise, frustration, or disappointment in informal settings, but not in polite company.

Shit Just Got Real

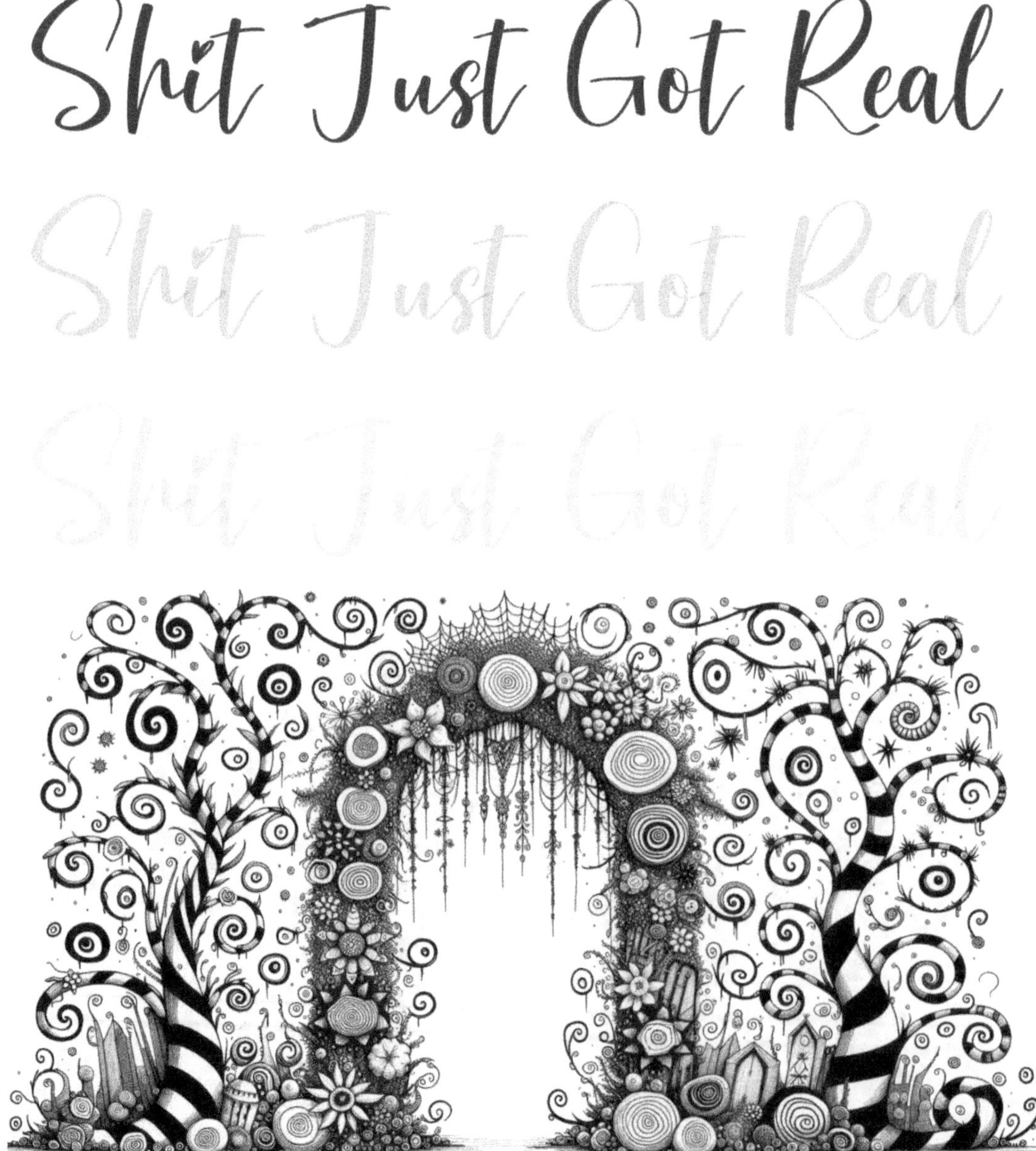

Wedding Program Header:

"Our Shitty Love Story Begins Now.

Our Shitty Love Story Begins Now

In Calligraphy: "Bith, Please!" - Suitable for a playful bachelorette party banner.
Daily Life: Use with caution among close friends when joking or teasing, but avoid in formal or professional conversations.

Bith Please!

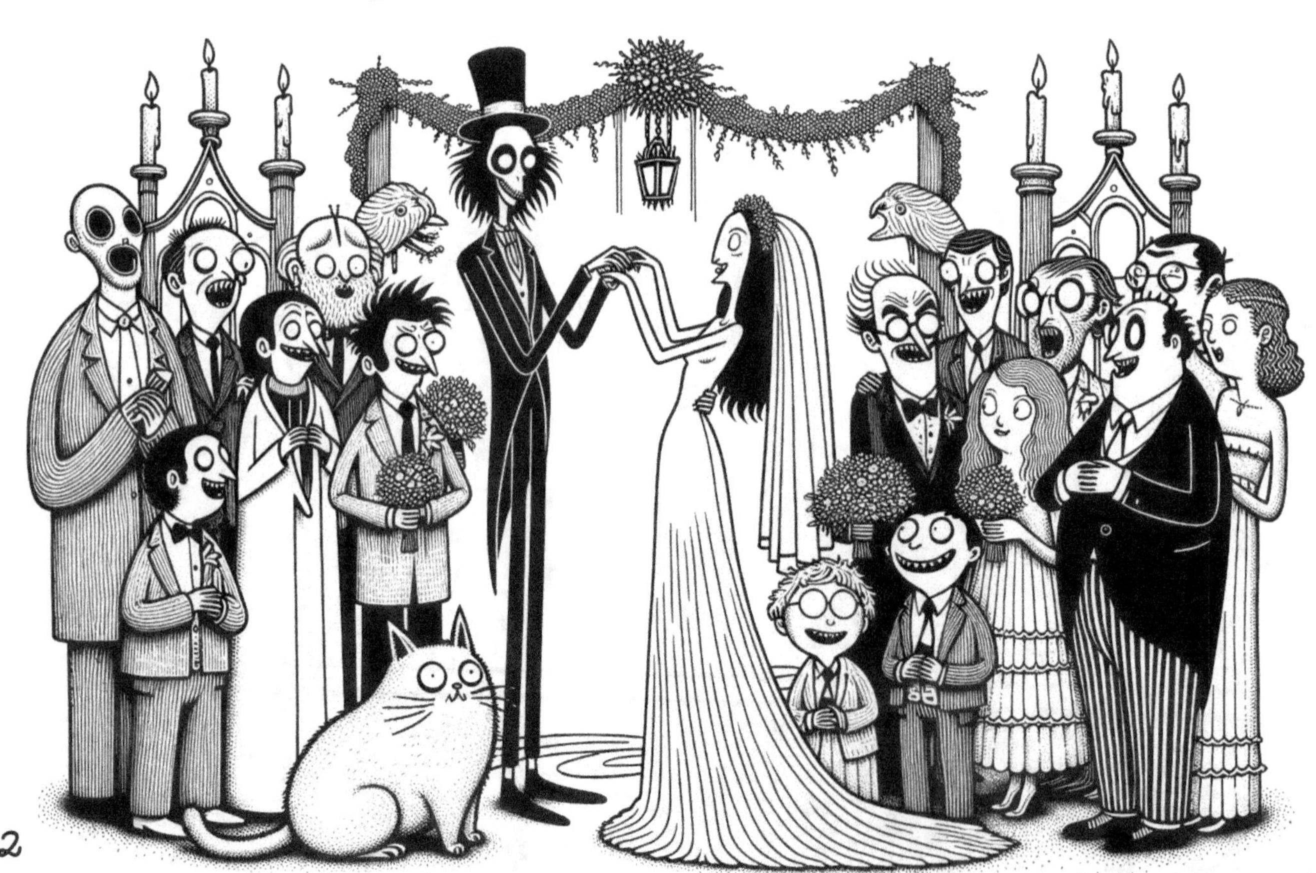

The Colorful A-Word:

In Calligraphy: "A Ass-Kicking Love" - Adds a touch of rebellion to a wedding reception sign.

Daily Life: Best used in casual conversations among friends or in situations where colorful language is accepted, but not in formal settings.

A Ass-Kicking Love

A Ass-Kicking Love

A Ass-Kicking Love

A Ass-Kicking Love

A Ass-Kicking Love

A Ass-Kicking Love

In Calligraphy: "Don't Give a Damn!" - Ideal for a carefree thank-you card message.

Daily Life: Use sparingly in informal conversations when expressing indifference or nonchalance, but avoid in professional or polite contexts.

Don't Give a Damn!

Don't Give a Damn!

Don't Give a Damn!

Don't Give a Damn!

Don't Give a Damn!

Don't Give a Damn!

In this section, we'll dive deep into the world of sassy and sarcastic calligraphy with a focus on perfecting the "Middle Finger Flourish." While traditional calligraphy may emphasize grace and elegance, our aim here is to add a touch of irreverence and attitude to your lettering.

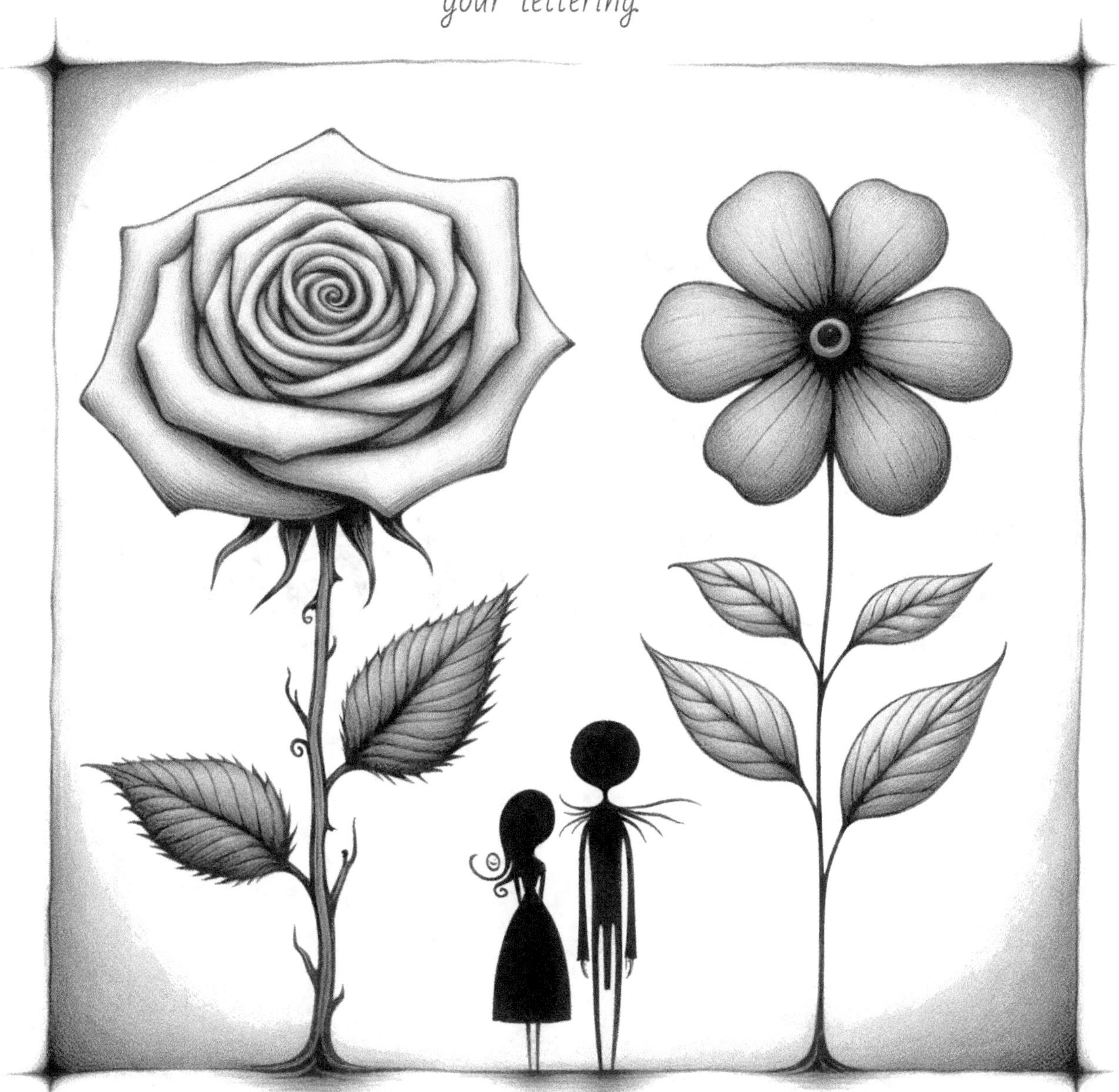

The Middle Finger Flourish: *A Gesture of Defiance*

The Middle Finger Flourish is a unique calligraphic technique that takes inspiration from one of the most universally recognized gestures of defiance and rebellion. It's a way to inject a bit of snark into your writing and make a bold statement. While it may not be suitable for all occasions, it's perfect for those who appreciate a good laugh and don't take themselves too seriously.

Creating Insulting Invitations, we'll explore some humorous and playful examples of wedding invitation wording with a sassy twist. Keep in mind that these examples are intended for fun and entertainment, so make sure your guests have a good sense of humor before using them for your actual wedding invitations.

Join Us You Lucky Bastards!
[Bride's Name] & [Groom's Name]
Are Getting Hitched!

Join Us You Lucky Bastards!
[Bride's Name] & [Groom's Name]
Are Getting Hitched!

Holy Shit
[Bride's Name] & [Groom's Name]
Are Finally Tying
the Fucking Knot!

Holy Shit
[Bride's Name] & [Groom's Name]
Are Finally Tying
the Fucking Knot!

You're Cordially Invited
to Witness
the Mother Fucking Wedding
of
[Bride's Name] & [Groom's Name]

You're Cordially Invited
to Witness
the Mother Fucking Wedding
of
[Bride's Name] & [Groom's Name]

Please RSVP by [Date]
to Secure Your Spot
at the Most Fucking Elegant
Event of the Year!

Please RSVP by [Date]
to Secure Your Spot
at the Most Fucking Elegant
Event of the Year!

Your Presence Is Requested
for an
Evening of Fine Dining
Excessive Drinking
and Shitty Dance Moves

Your Presence Is Requested
for an
Evening of Fine Dining
Excessive Drinking
and Shitty Dance Moves

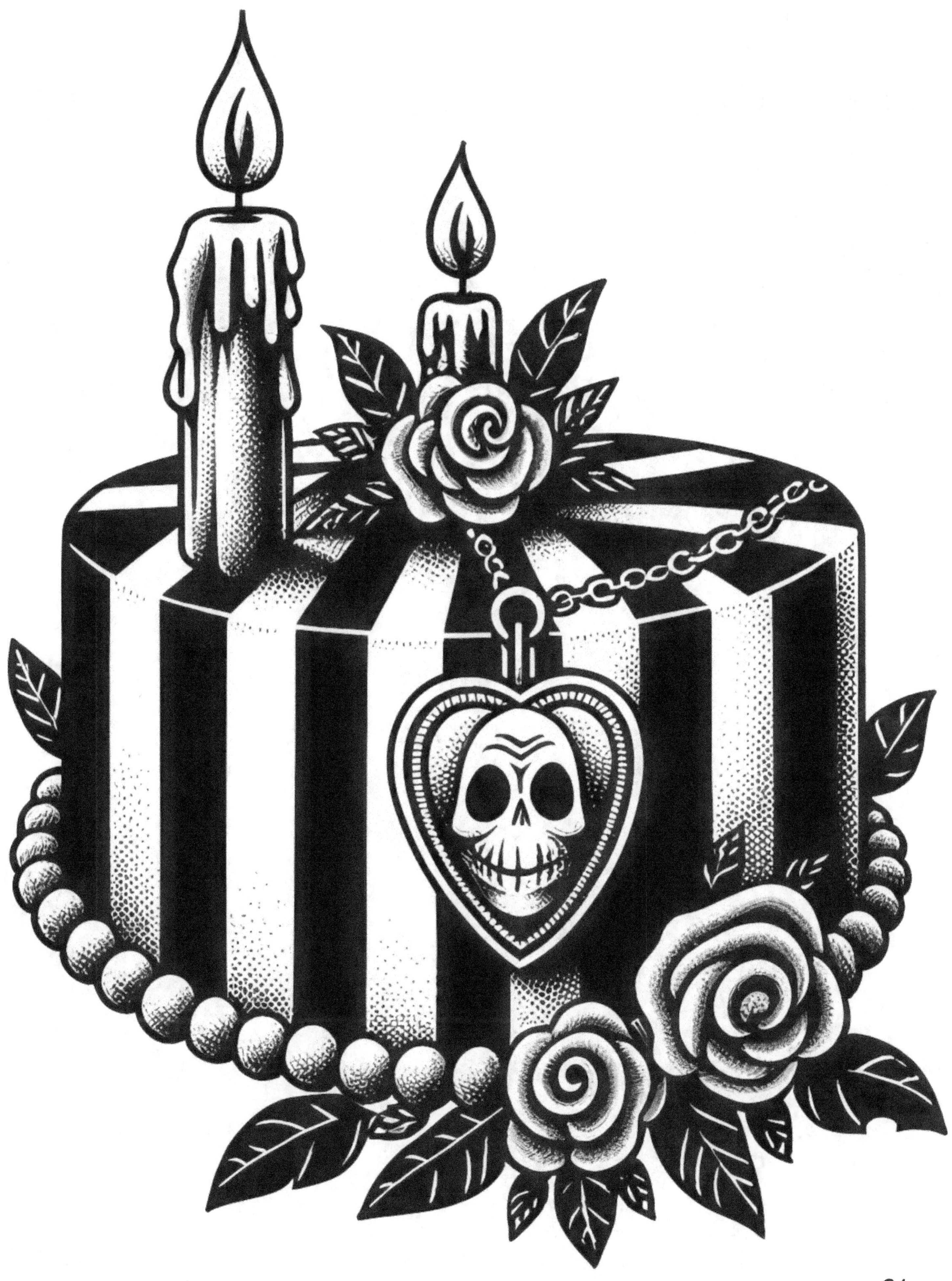

Together with Their Families
[Bride's Name] & [Groom's Name]
Invite You to the Wedding
of the Fucking Century

Together with Their Families
[Bride's Name] & [Groom's Name]
Invite You to the Wedding
of the Fucking Century

We're Doing This Thing!
[Bride's Name] & [Groom's Name]
Would Love for You to Share
in the Fucking Joy

We're Doing This Thing!
[Bride's Name] & [Groom's Name]
Would Love for You to Share
in the Fucking Joy

Put on Your Fancy Parts
and Join Us as
[Bride's Name] & [Groom's Name]
Say 'Fuck Yeah' to Forever!

Put on Your Fancy Parts
and Join Us as
[Bride's Name] & [Groom's Name]
Say 'Fuck Yeah' to Forever!

It's Happening, People!
[Bride's Name] & [Groom's Name]
Are Getting Hitched
So Bring Your A-Game
and Your Sense of Humor!

It's Happening, People!
[Bride's Name] & [Groom's Name]
Are Getting Hitched
So Bring Your A-Game
and Your Sense of Humor!

These examples should give you a taste of the playful and sassy approach to wedding invitations. Feel free to adapt them to your own style and preferences, and remember to ensure that your guests will appreciate the humor before sending them out.

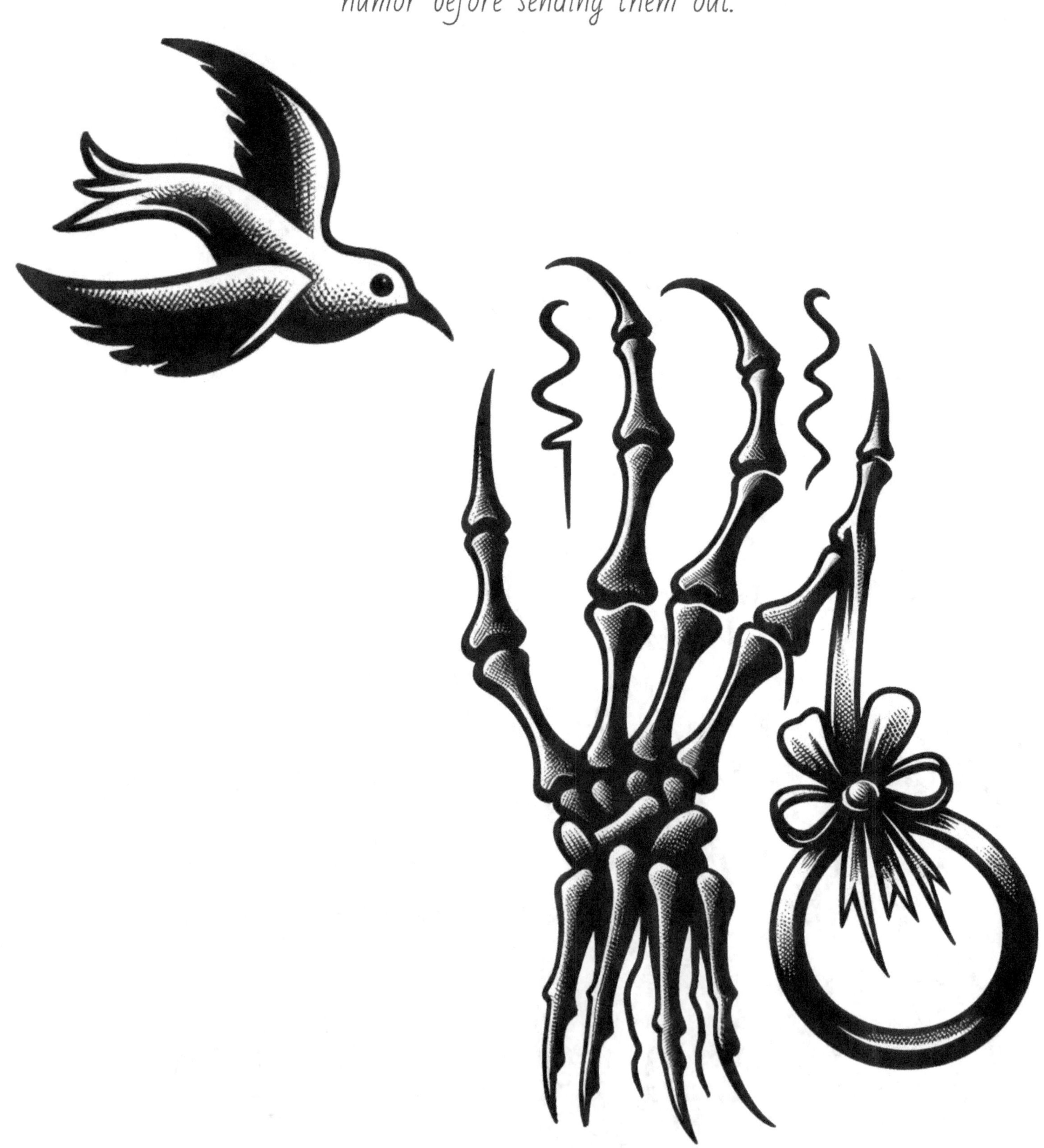

Monograms and More, we'll explore some examples of monograms and decorative elements with a sassy and humorous twist. These examples can add a unique and playful touch to your wedding decor and stationery.

Introducing the Shit! tastic Monogram of

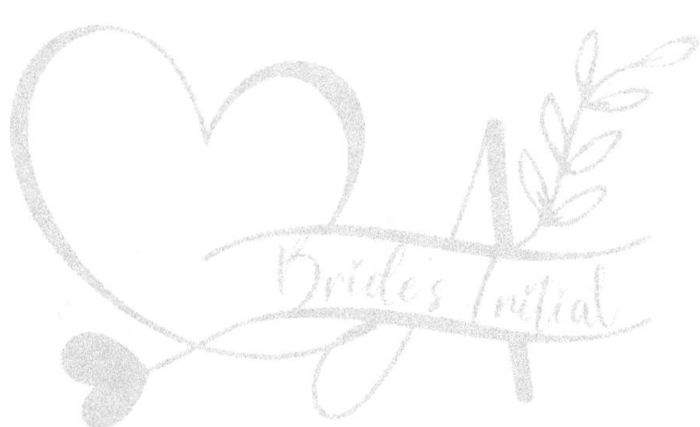

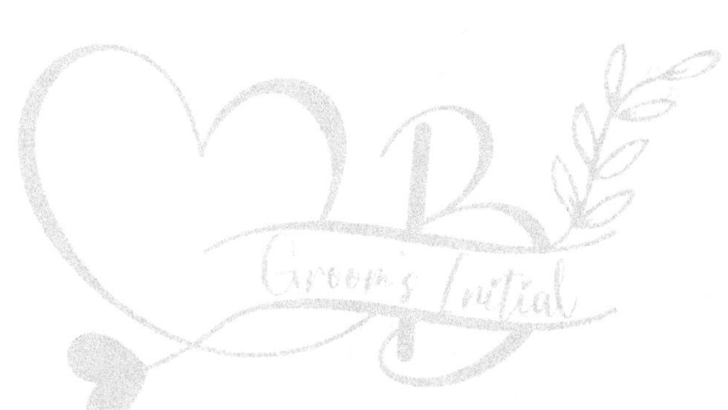

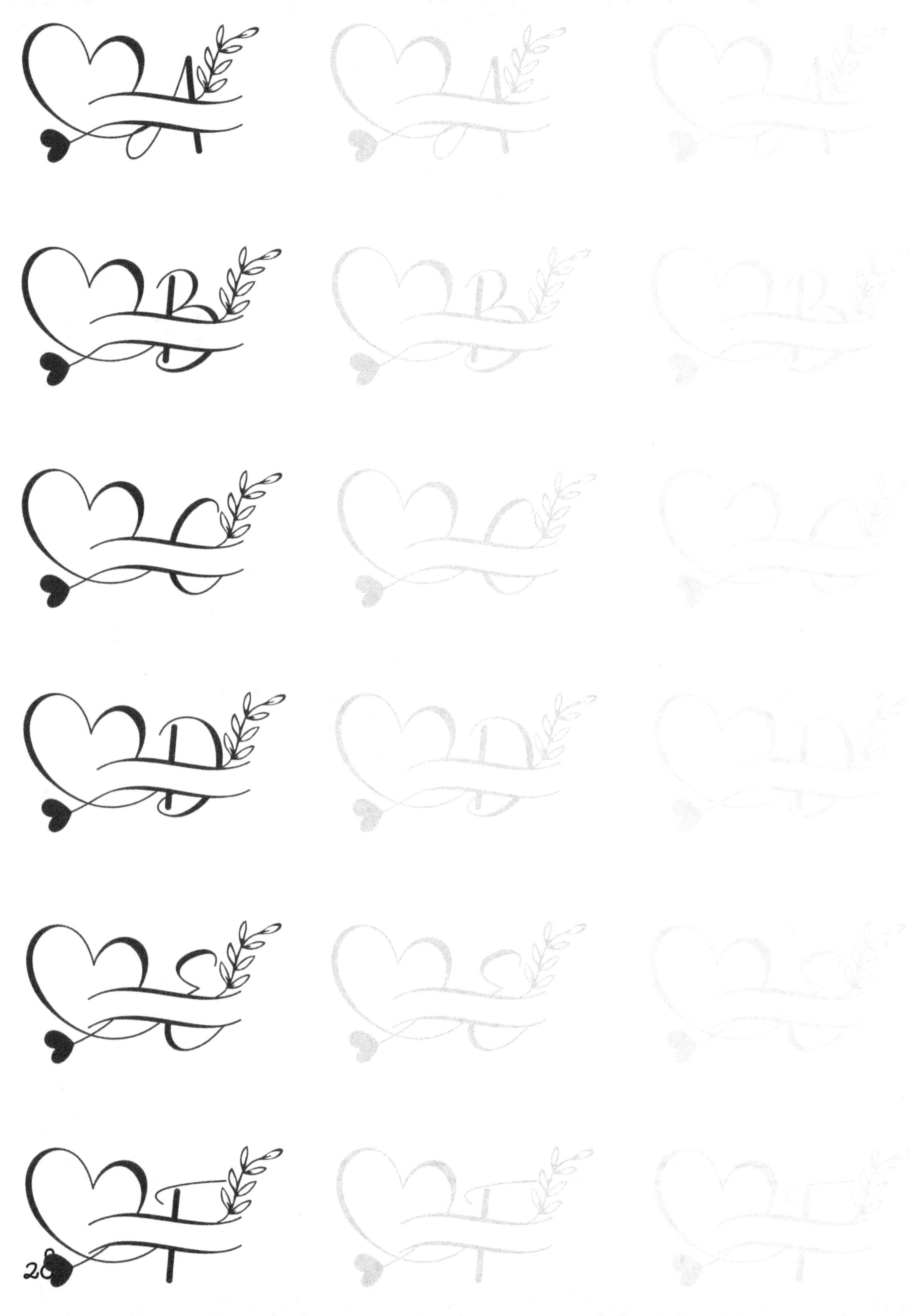

28

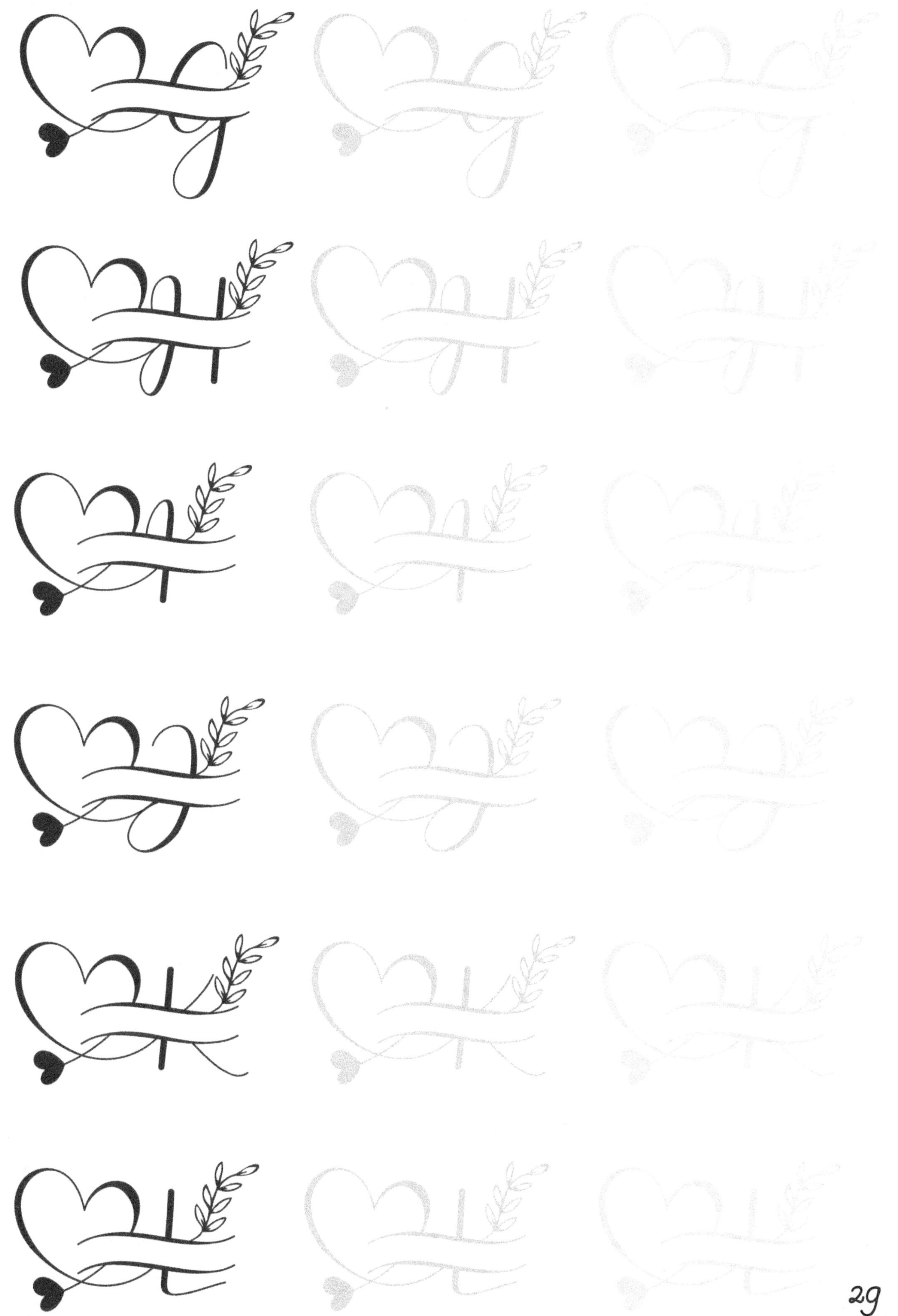

29

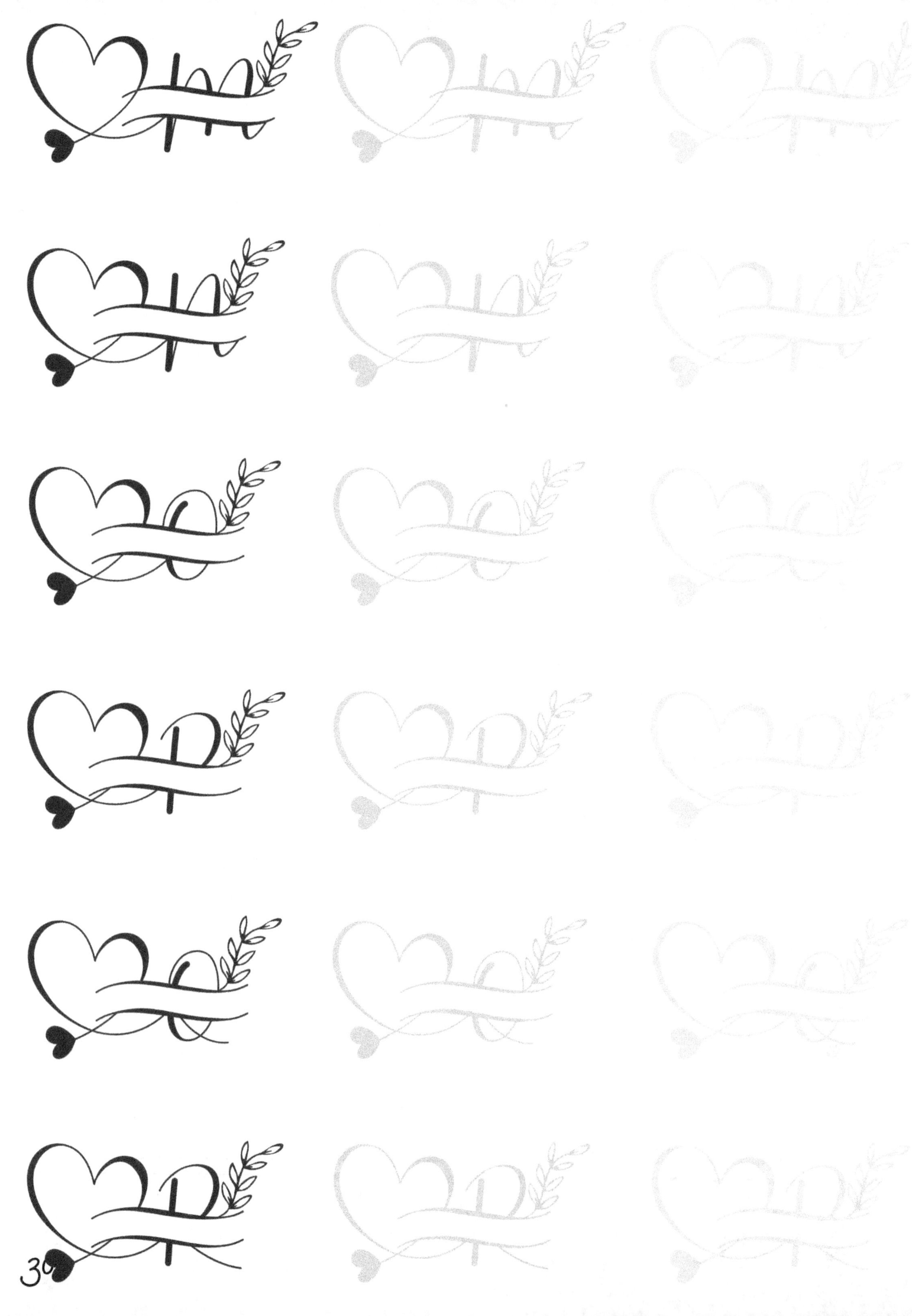

30

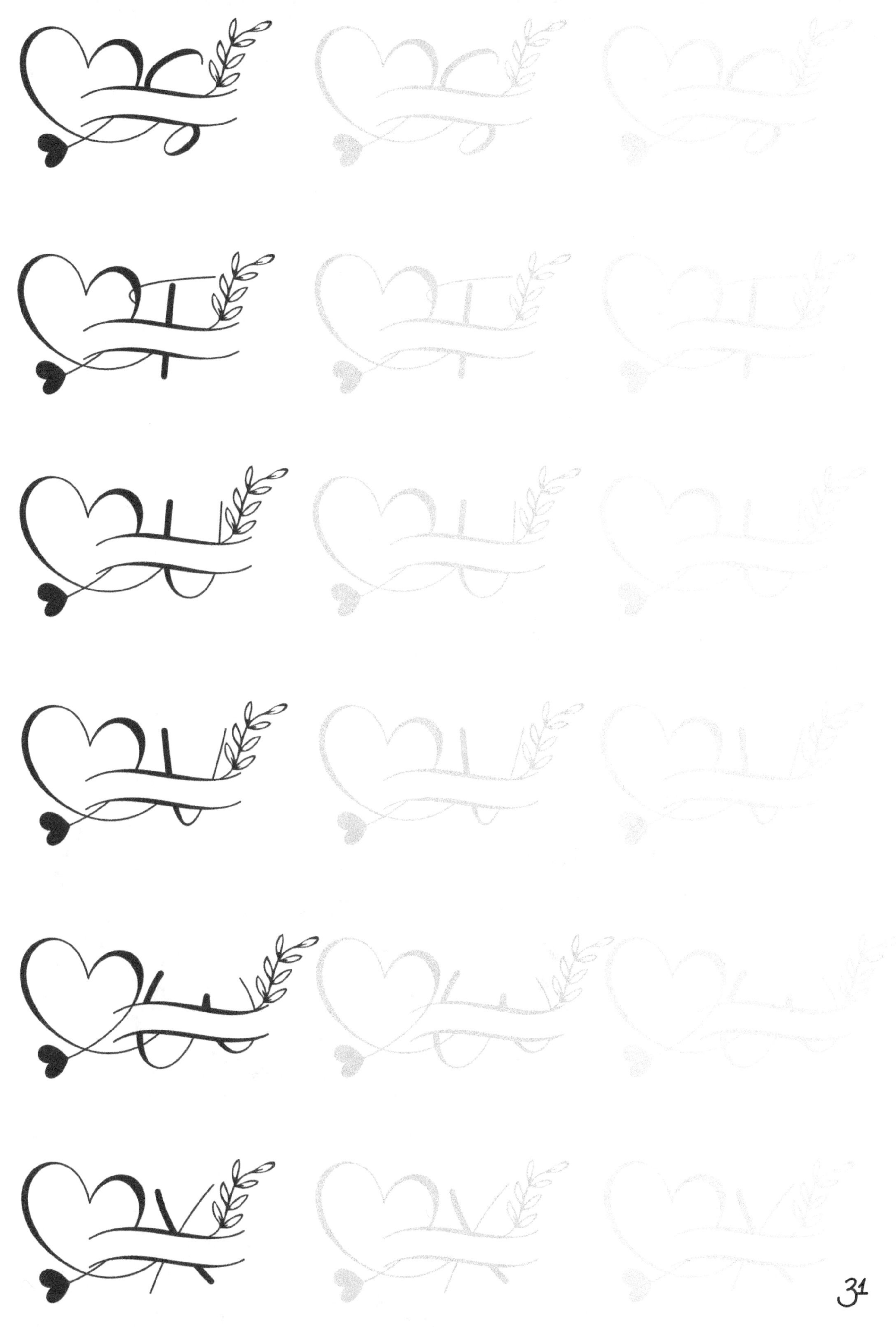

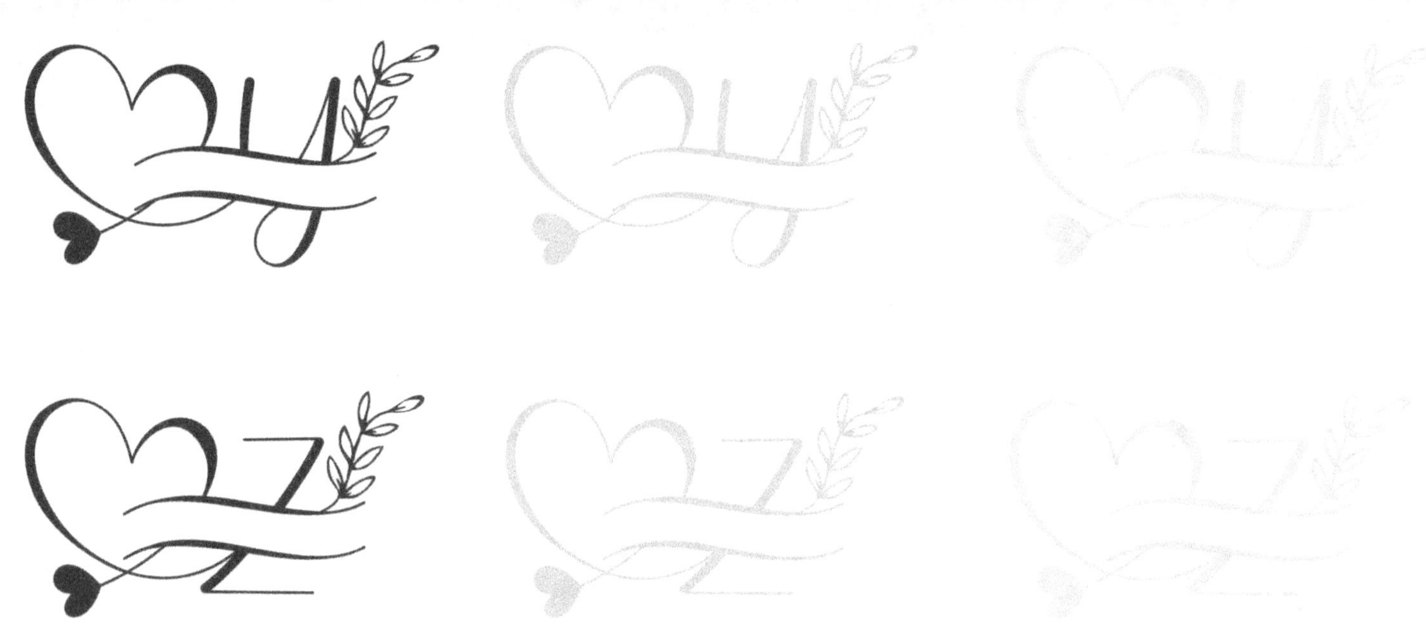

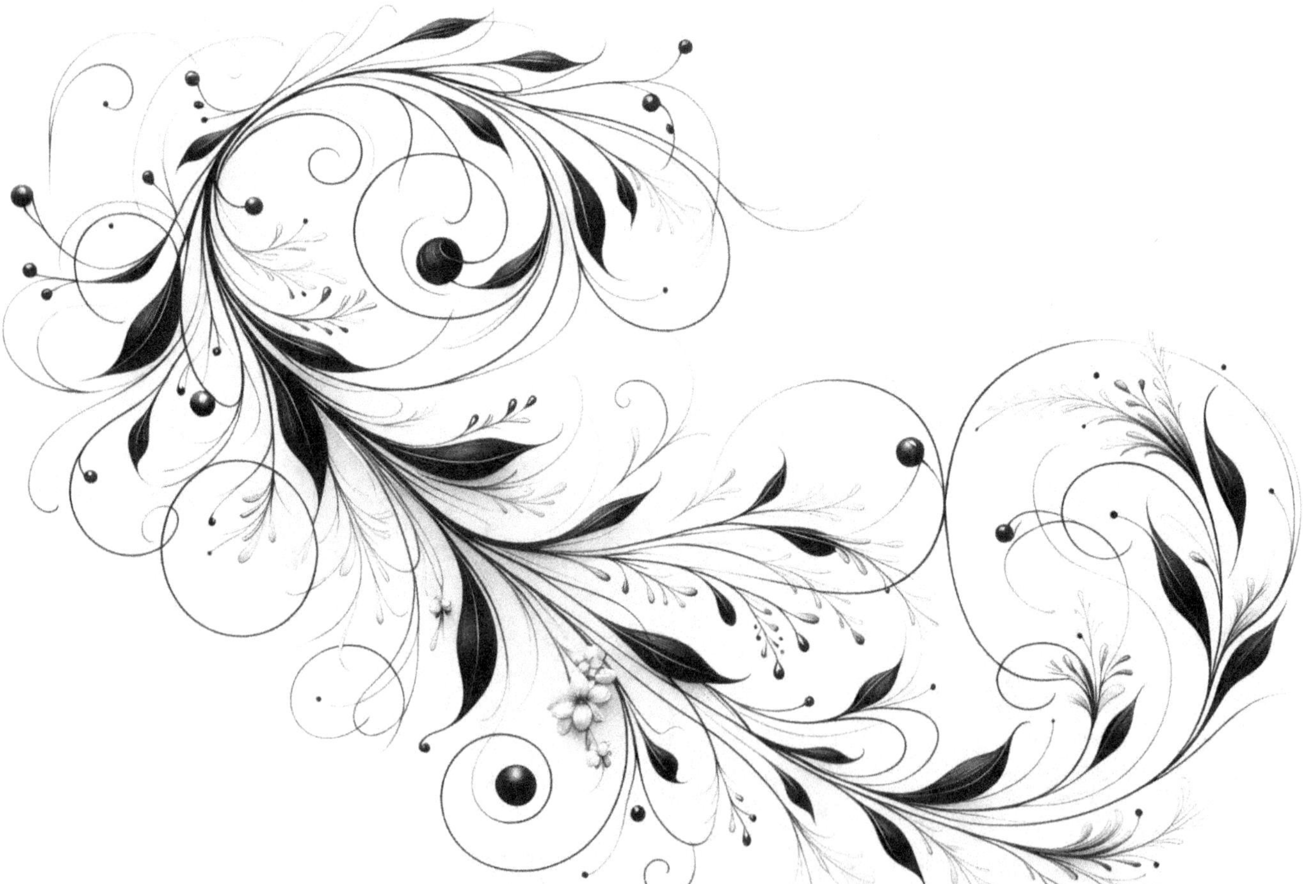

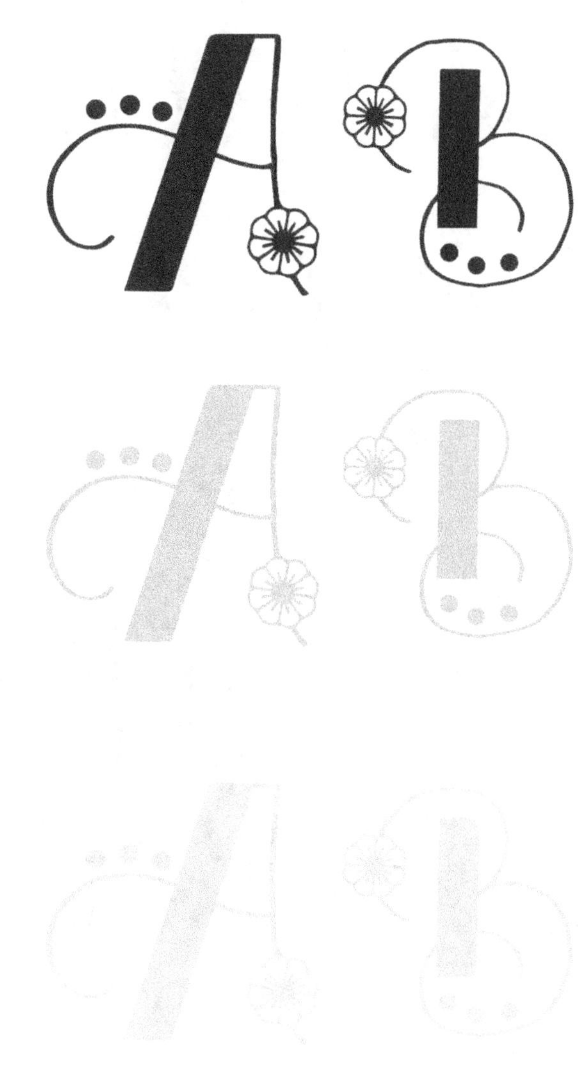

Because Our Love Couldn't Get Any More Fucking Official

Get Ready for the Most Elegant Motherf Fucking Monogram You've Ever Seen!

 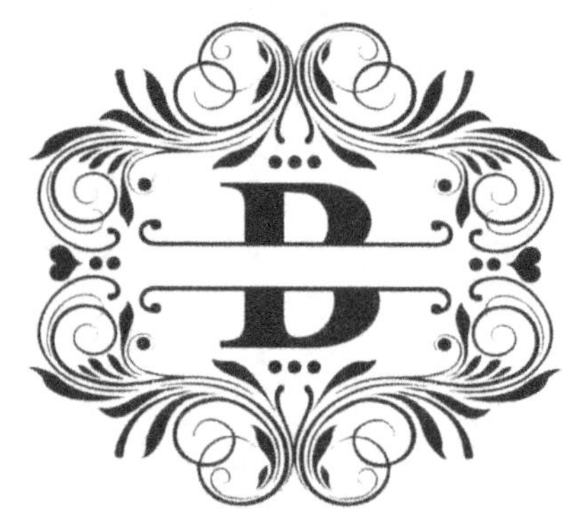

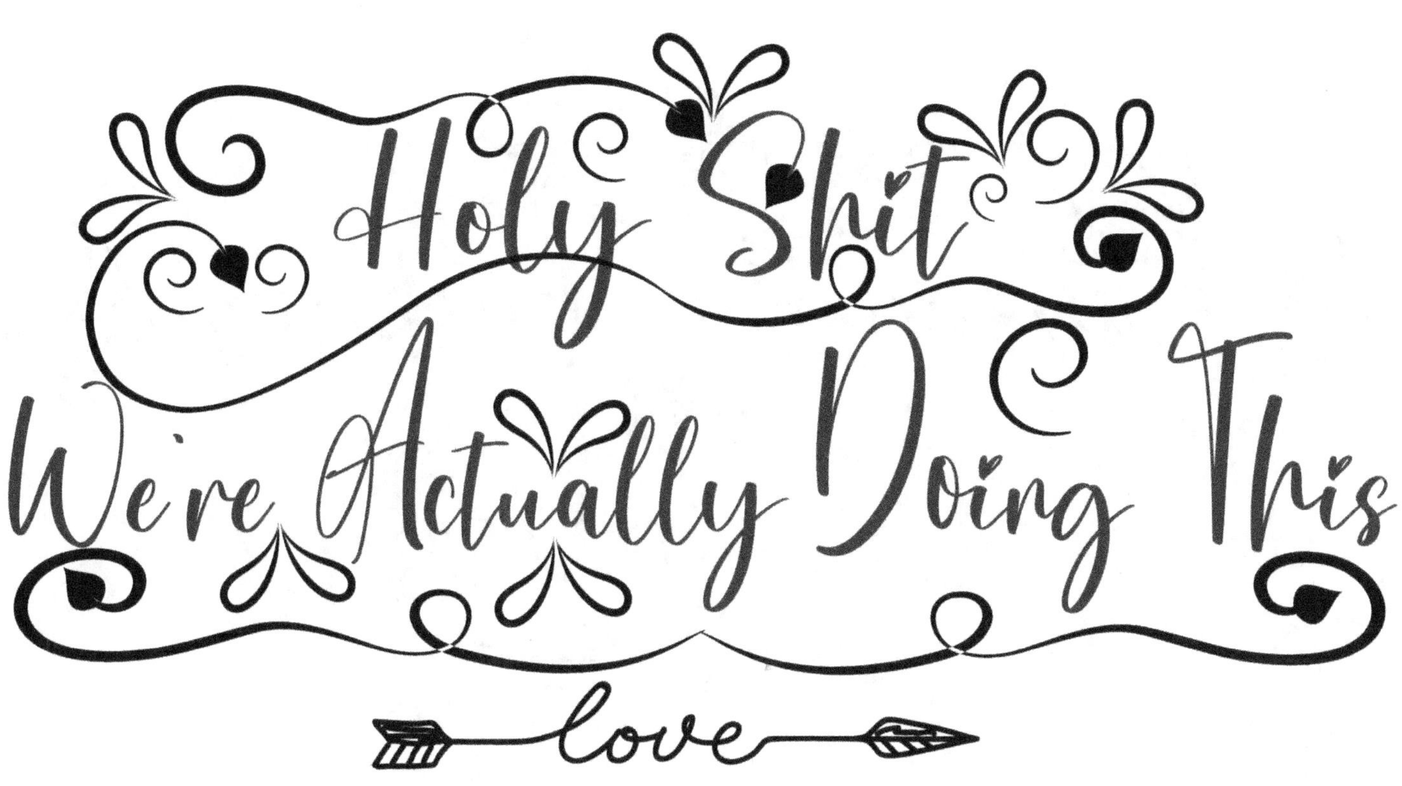
Holy Shit
We're Actually Doing This
love

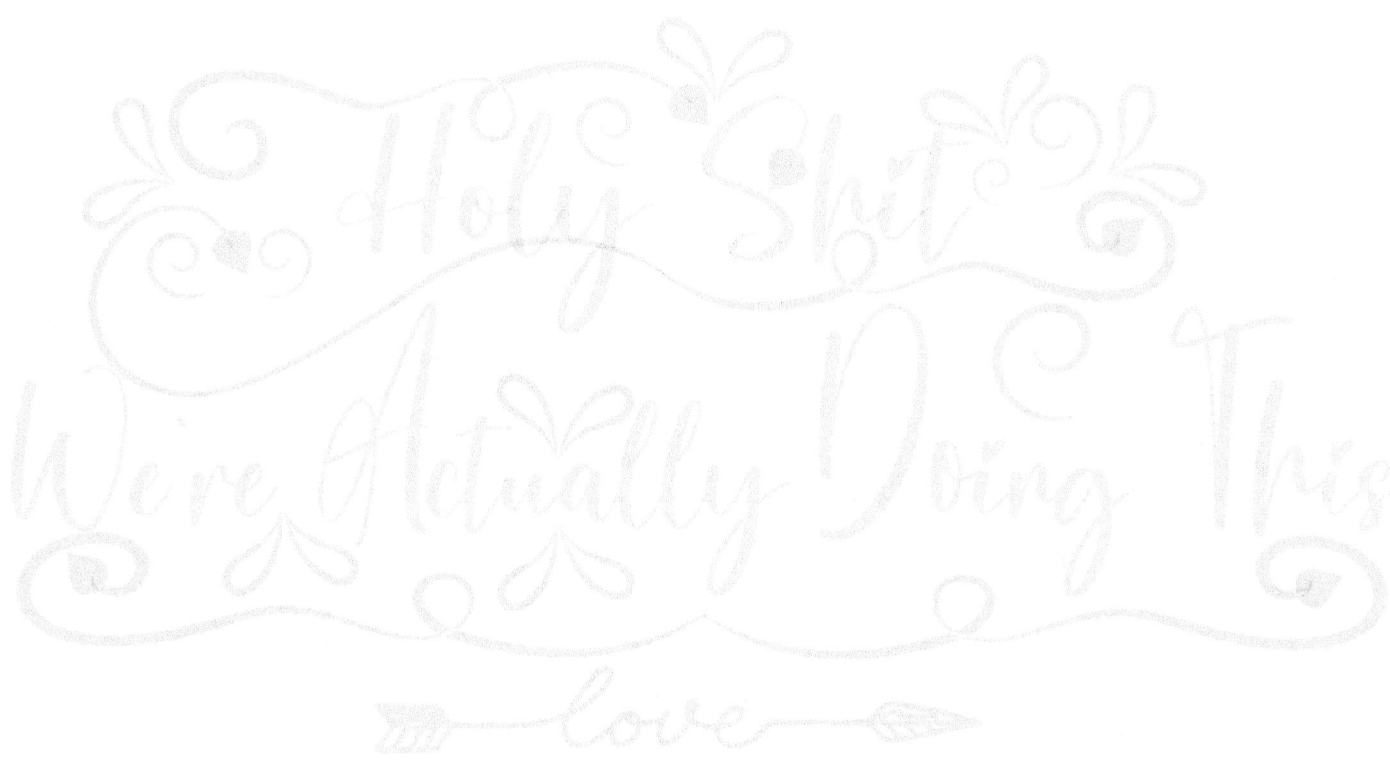
Holy Shit
We're Actually Doing This
love

Putting the Fucking Wow in Vow

Flourishing Our Way into Matrimonial Disaster

Holy Shit
We're Actually Doing This

love

Flourishing Our Way
into
Matrimonial Disaster

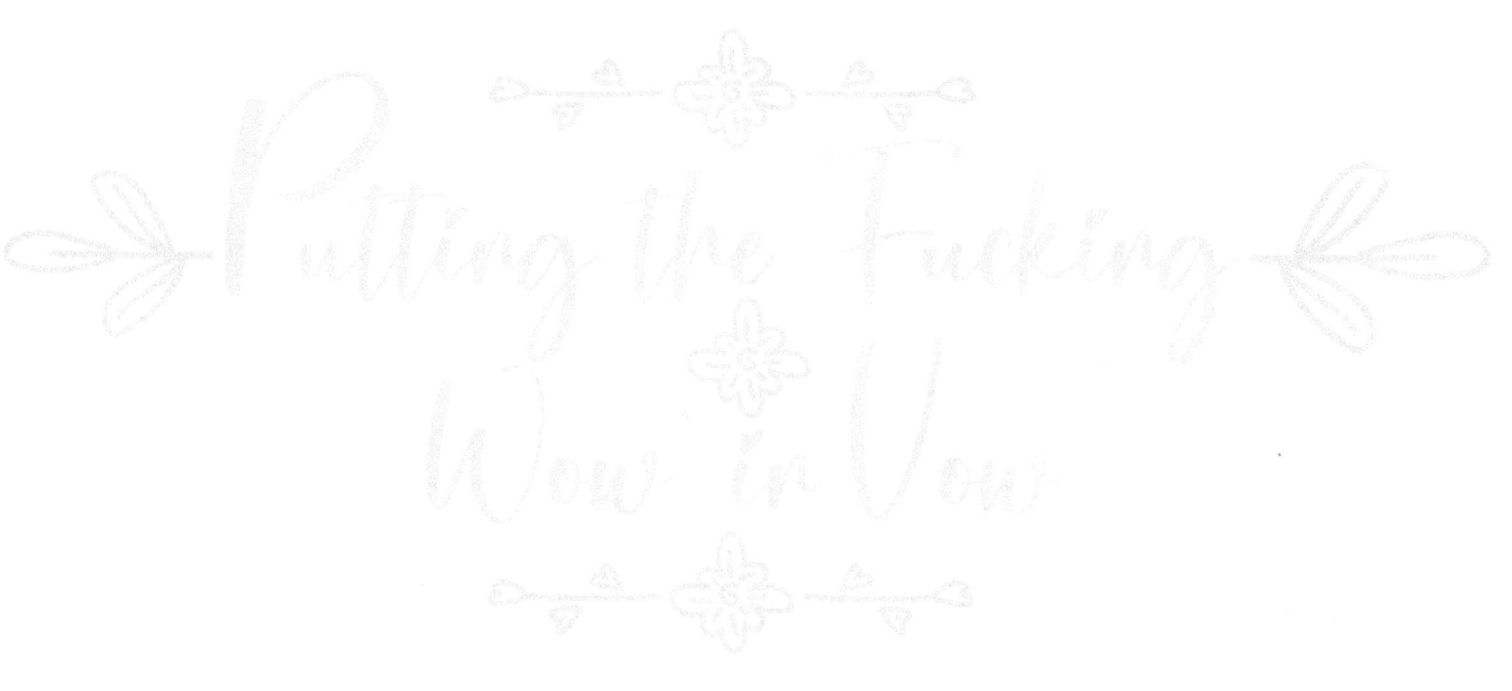
Putting the Fucking
Wow in Vow

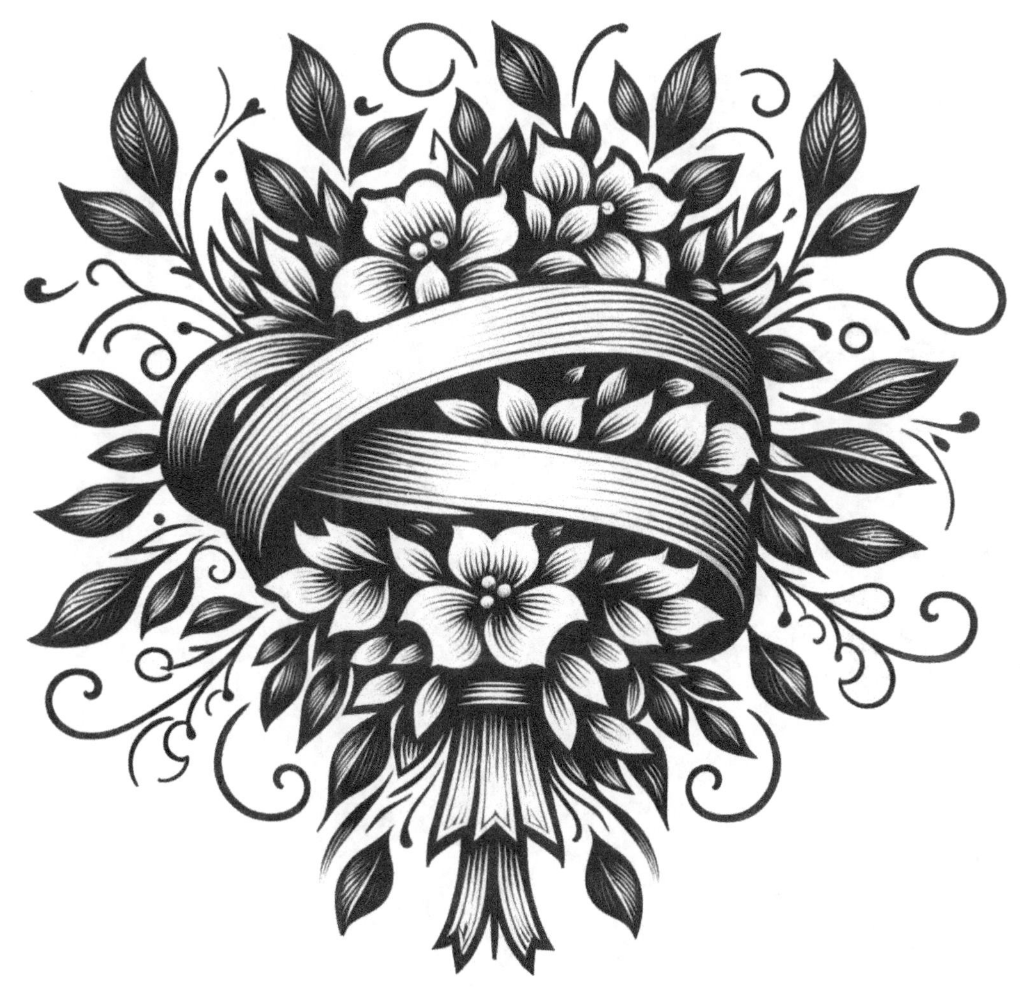

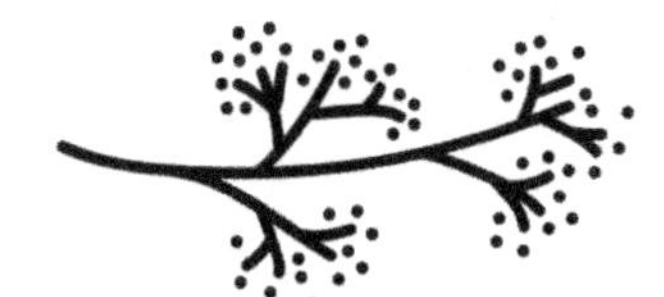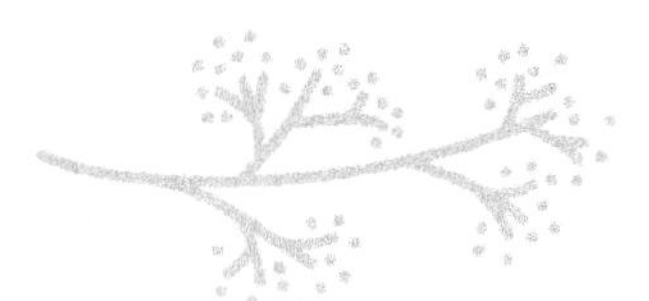

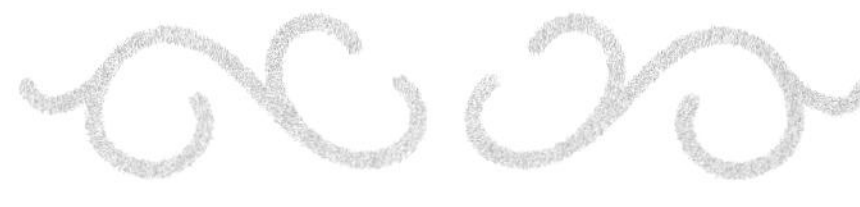

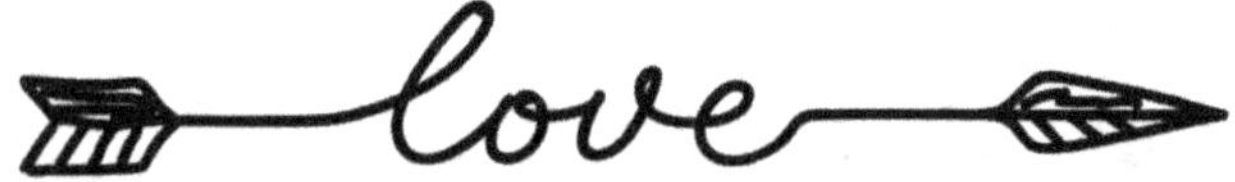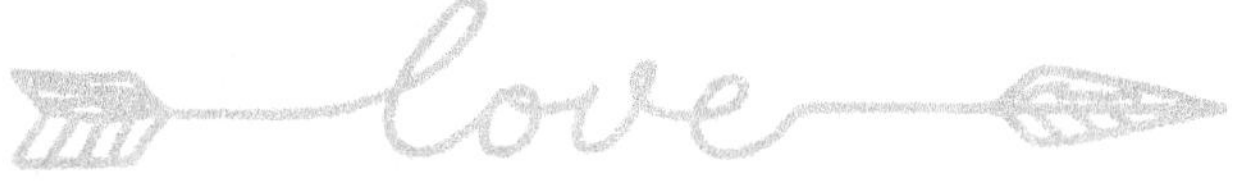

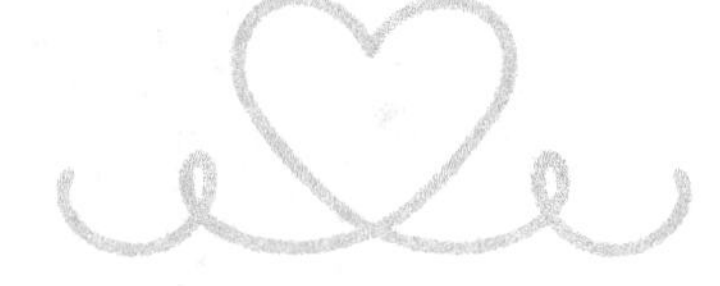

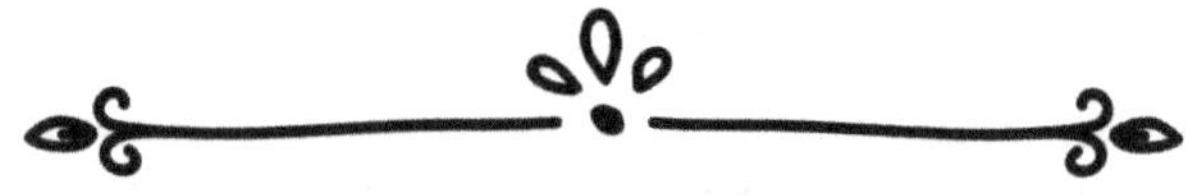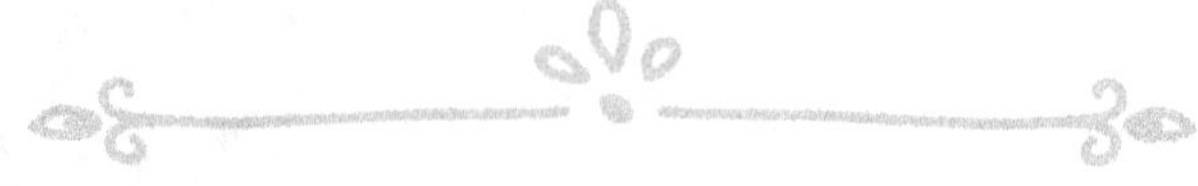

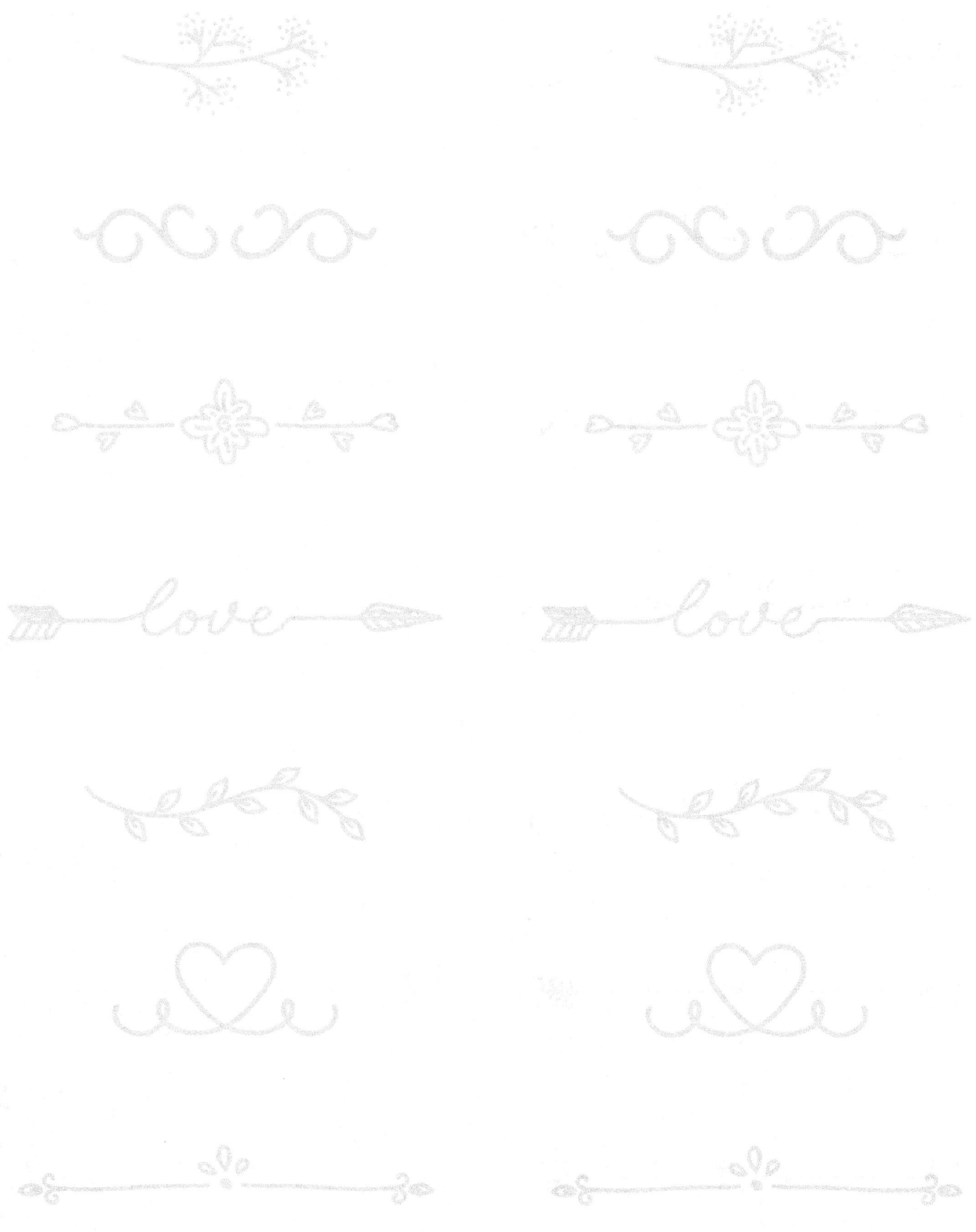

love
love

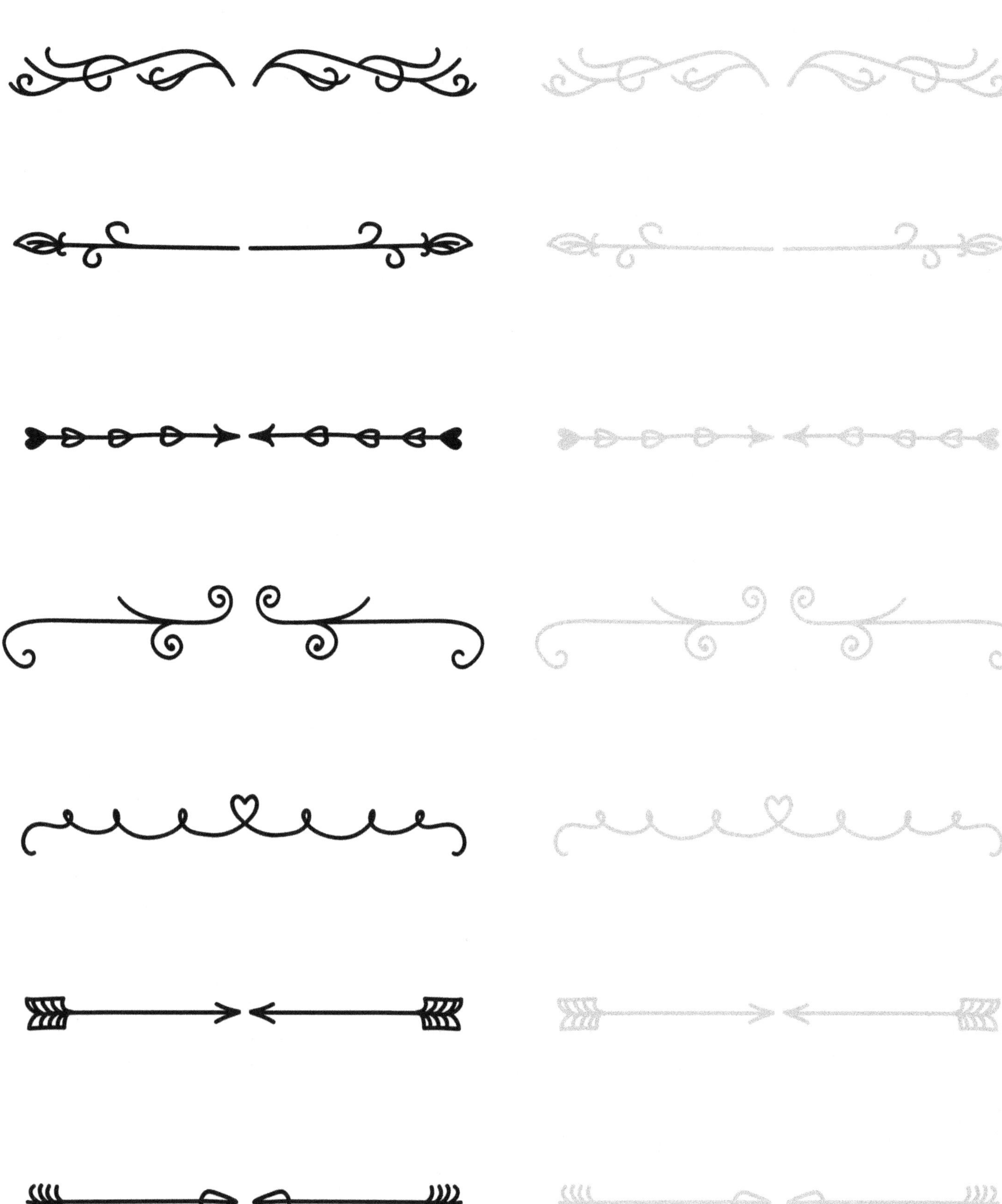

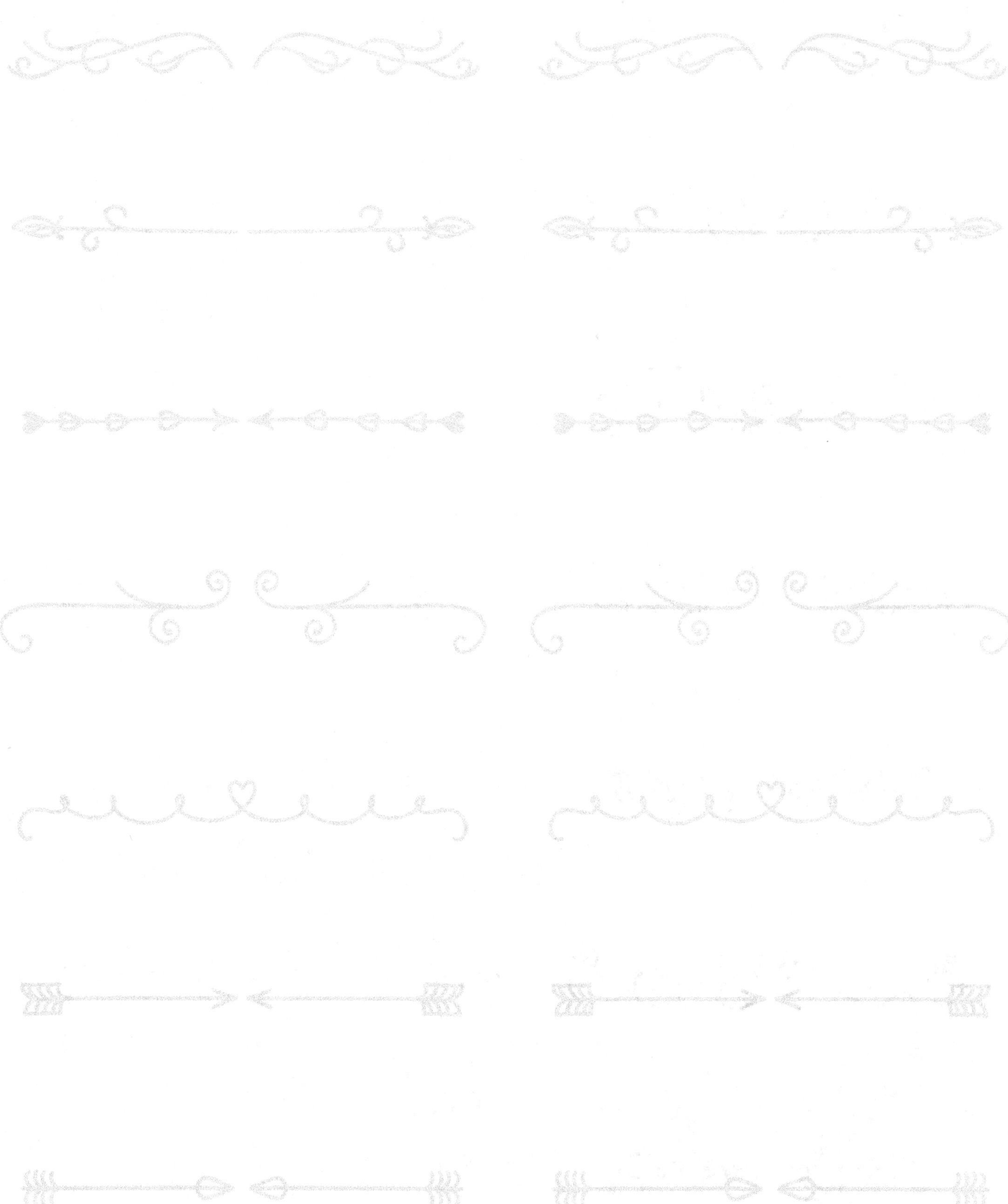

13: „Dress Up Your Wedding Venue with Our Fucking Fantastic Decorations"

This slogan can be employed as a headline for a welcome sign that greets guests as they enter the wedding venue. It sets the tone for a ceremony that's anything but conventional. Think of incorporating flourishes that are both elegant and audacious around the text. Use techniques such as oversized capitals or ornamental strokes to make the word Fucking really stand out, and create an appealing visual contrast with the rest of the text.

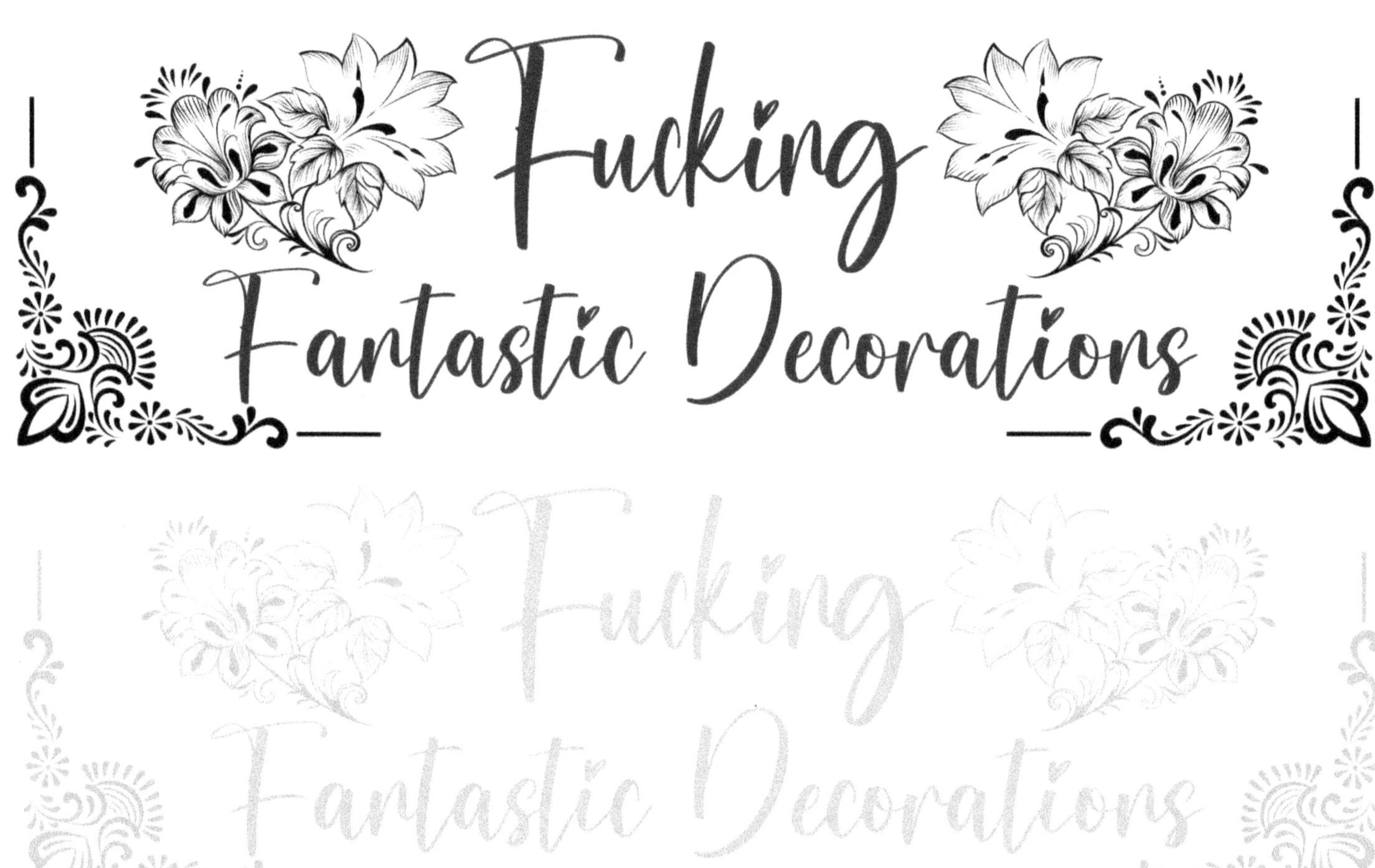

Techniques to Consider:

Chiaroscuro Shading: Make those flourishes pop with some intense darks and lights.

Pointed Pen Variations: Use this for the word "Fantastic" to make it look as epic as it sounds.

Flourished Borders: Surround the text with a border of intricate flourishes that are as elaborate as they are cheeky.

2.3: "Prepare to Be Amazed by the Sassy Decorations of [Bride's Name) & [Groom's Name)

This slogan is ideal for either an invitation or a program guide, serving as a teaser for what's to come. Here, you can play around with "swashes" and "loops" to create a sense of anticipation and whimsy. The words "Prepare to Be Amazed" can be accentuated with exaggerated ascenders and descenders, with flourishes that defy gravity.

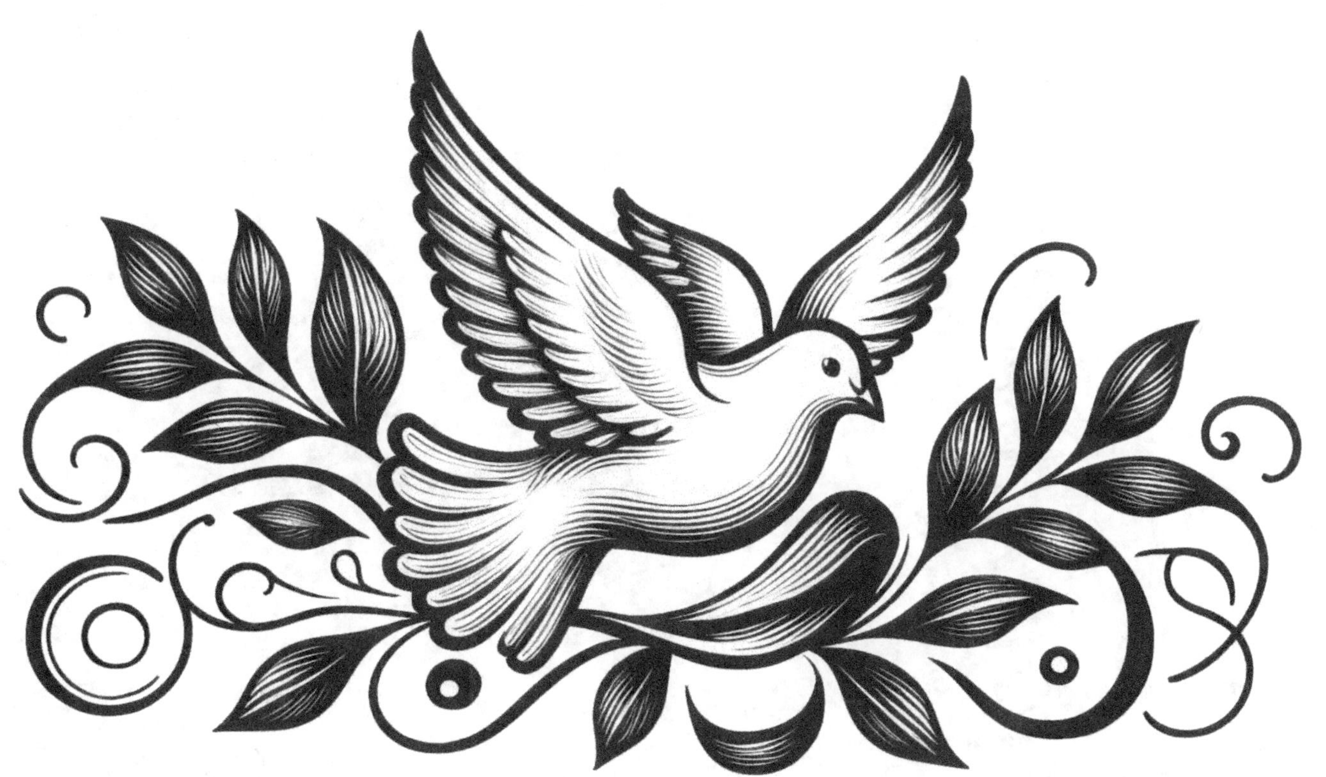

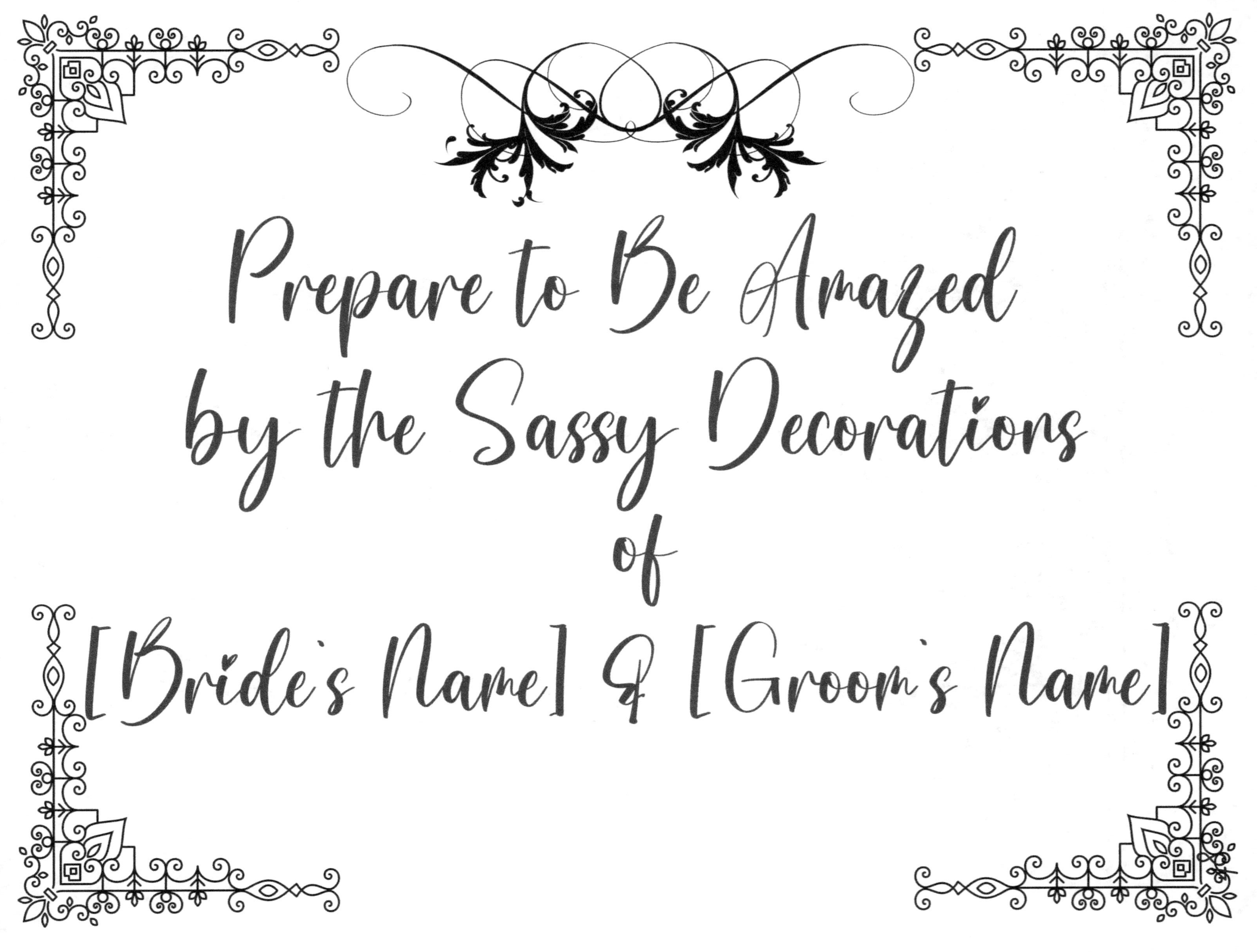

Prepare to Be Amazed
by the Sassy Decorations
of
[Bride's Name] & [Groom's Name]

Prepare to Be Amazed
by the Sassy Decorations
of
[Bride's Name] & [Groom's Name]

Varying Text Sizes: Use hierarchy to focus on the important words, such as "Decorate," "Celebrate," and "Laugh."

Rhythmic Spacing: Create a visual rhythm by altering the spacing between different elements of the text.

Ligature Play: Use ligatures creatively to connect and emphasize words that are vital to the message.

"Decorate, Celebrate, and Don't Forget to Laugh: [Bride's Name) & [Groom's Name) Do It in Style!

This one is a call to action, a perfect tagline for a series of event signs or even for the dance floor. Given the longer text, careful planning is needed to ensure readability while still allowing room for decorative elements.

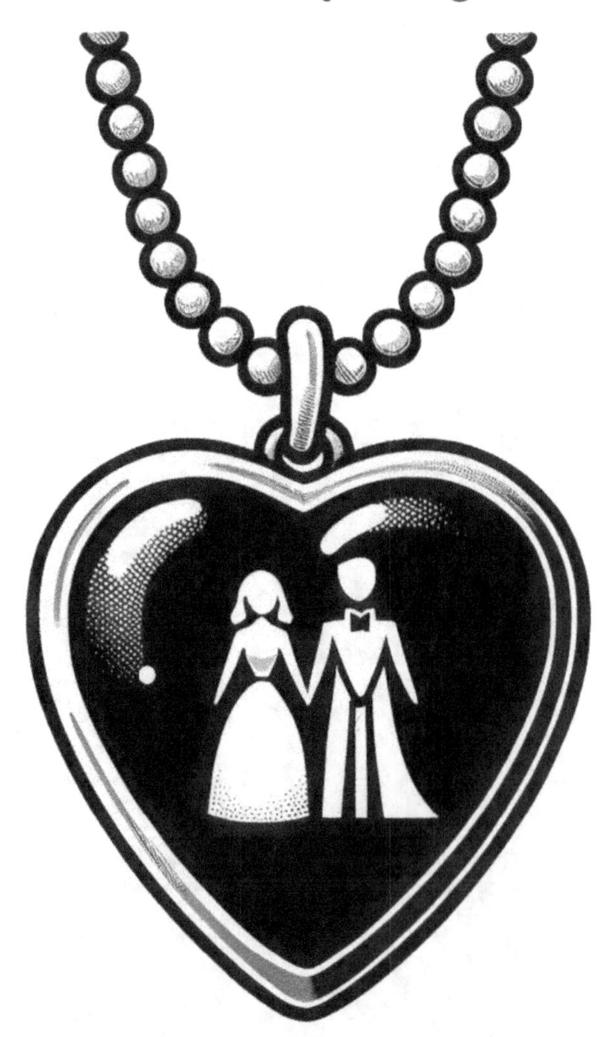

Decorate, Celebrate,
and
Don't Forget to Laugh
[Bride's Name] & [Groom's Name]
Do It in Style!

Decorate, Celebrate,
and
Don't Forget to Laugh
[Bride's Name] & [Groom's Name]
Do It in Style!

Chapter 5: Practicing Your Potty-Mouth Penmanship
Introduction

In this chapter, we'll focus on the practical exercises that will help you master the art of profane calligraphy. From daily drills to love letters with a twist, we'll guide you through a series of exercises designed to improve your skill and expand your vulgar vocabulary.

Daily practice is essential for mastering any form of calligraphy, and profanity-laden script is no exception. In this section, we'll introduce a set of drills that incorporate swear words, allowing you to practice both your penmanship and your profanity.

Practical Tips and Examples:

Drill 1: Basic Strokes with Cuss Words

Practice the fundamental strokes of your chosen calligraphy style, but replace the standard characters with swear words. For example, practice the Copperplate oval shape by writing the word "Shit!" repeatedly.

Shit Shit Shit Shit Shit

Shit Shit Shit Shit Shit

Shit Shit Shit Shit

Shit Shit Shit Shit Shit

Shit Shit Shit Shit

Shit Shit Shit Shit Shit

Drill 2: *Ligature Practice*

Work on connecting swear words in a fluid and elegant manner. For instance, practice writing "Fucking Amazing" focusing on the ligature between g and A.

Fucking Amazing

Fucking Amazing

Fucking Amazing

Fucking Amazing

Fucking Amazing

Drill 3: *Flourishing with Profanity*

Add flourishes to your swear words to make them stand out. For example, add a dramatic tail to the D in "Damn" or a loop to the F in "Fuck".

Damn *Damn Damn Damn*

Damn Damn Damn Damn

Damn Damn Damn Damn

Fuck *Fuck Fuck Fuck Fuck*

Fuck Fuck Fuck Fuck Fuck

Fuck Fuck Fuck Fuck Fuck

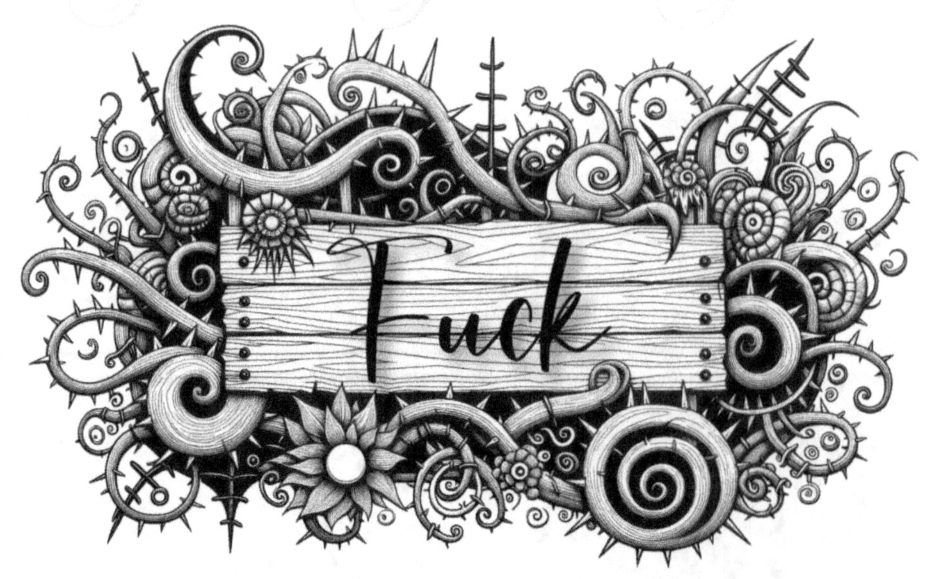

Section 5.2: Writing Love Letters with a Twist

Love letters are a classic application of calligraphy, but in this section, we'll add a profane twist. Learn how to express affection and irreverence simultaneously through the medium of ink

Practical Tips and Examples

Example 1: The Romantic Rant

Start with a traditional love letter opening, such as "My Dearest," but follow it with a string of profanities that are endearing in context. For example:

My Dearest,
You are the Fucking light of my life.

My Dearest,
You are the Fucking light of my life.

My Dearest,
You are the Fucking light of my life.

To the one who Fucking completes me, every damn day feels like a blessing with you.

To the one who Fucking completes me, every damn day feels like a blessing with you.

To the one who Fucking completes me, every damn day feels like a blessing with you.

Darling,
out of all the people in this world,
you're my absolute favorite
pain in the ass.

Darling,
out of all the people in this world,
you're my absolute favorite
pain in the ass.

Write a short poem where every other line contains a swear word, but the overall tone is romantic. For instance:

Roses are red,
This love isn't Shit,
Violets are blue,
I Fucking love you.

Roses are red,
This love isn't Shit,
Violets are blue,
I Fucking love you.

Your touch, it sets my soul aflame,
This Fucking love, I can't tame.
With every glance, with every sigh,
I'm damn sure you're my kind of guy.

Your touch, it sets my soul aflame,
This Fucking love, I can't tame.
With every glance, with every sigh,
I'm damn sure you're my kind of guy.

Our love story, wild and free,
Is Fucking perfect, can't you see?
Through thick and thin,
through joy and strife,
I'll Fucking love you, all my life.

Our love story, wild and free,
Is Fucking perfect, can't you see?
Through thick and thin,
through joy and strife,
I'll Fucking love you, all my life.

I can't Fucking imagine
my life without you

I can't Fucking imagine
my life without you

I can't Fucking imagine
my life without you

I can't Fucking imagine
my life without you

Section 61: The Invitations that Made Guests Say "WTF?"

Introduction:

Wedding invitations are the first glimpse guests get into the theme and tone of your wedding. For couples looking to infuse a touch of humor and edginess into their big day, a profanity-laced invitation can be just the ticket. But how do you strike the right balance between shock and sophistication? Let's dive into some real-life examples that nailed it.

1.The Bold Announcement:

One couple decided to forgo the traditional "You're cordially invited" for a more direct "You're Fucking Invited!" The elegant script and high-quality paper gave it a touch of class, while the bold statement set the tone for a fun and unconventional wedding.

2. The Playful RSVP:

Another memorable invitation featured an RSVP card with the options:

"Hell Yes!"

"Damn, Can't Make It."

"Will Decide at the Last Fucking Minute."

This playful approach gave guests a chuckle and set the stage for a laid-back celebration.

3 The Subtle Hint:

For couples wanting a more subtle approach, one invitation featured a beautifully drawn bird, with the caption, "This bird has a message for you." On closer inspection, the bird was subtly flipping the bird. It was a cheeky nod for those in the know, without being too in-your-face.

4. The Rhyming Revelry:

A poetic couple sent out invitations with a limerick:
"Two lovers are tying the knot,
In a venue that costs quite a lot.
So come join the spree,
And RSVP,
Or we'll think you're a total afterthought."

5. The Straightforward Save-the-Date:

One save-the-date card simply read, "Mark the Fucking Date!" with the wedding details below. The minimalist design and bold statement made it a memorable piece that guests were sure to pin to their fridge.

Tips for Crafting Your Own Profane Invitation:

Know Your Audience: Make sure your guests will appreciate the humor and not be offended.

Quality Matters: Using high-quality materials and elegant design can offset the shock of the profanity and make it feel more intentional.

Be Authentic: Your invitation should reflect you and your partner's personalities. If you're naturally cheeky and playful, let that shine through. If not, consider a more subtle approach.

Conclusion:

Incorporating profanity into your wedding invitation can be a fun and memorable way to set the tone for your big day. Whether you go bold and brash or subtle and cheeky, the key is to be authentic and considerate of your audience. After all, you want your guests to be excited about your wedding, not put off by the invitation.

Introduction:

Place cards may seem like a minor detail in the grand scheme of a wedding, but they offer a unique opportunity to inject personality and humor into your event. For couples looking to add a touch of cheekiness to their table settings, profanity-laced place cards can be a delightful surprise for guests. Let's explore some real-life examples that brought the pizzazz.

1. The Direct Address:

One couple opted for a straightforward approach with their place cards, addressing each guest with a playful "Sit Your Ass Down, [Guest's Name)." The unexpected directive, combined with a classy font and elegant cardstock, struck the perfect balance between humor and formality.

Sit Your Ass Down, [Guest's Name]

Another set of place cards took a more complimentary route, addressing guests
with phrases like:

The Fucking Fabulous
[Guest's Name]

The Fucking Fabulous
[Guest's Name]

The Damn Delightful
[Guest's Name]

The Damn Delightful
[Guest's Name]

The Bloody Brilliant [Guest's Name]

The Bloody Brilliant [Guest's Name]

This approach not only added humor but also made each guest feel special and appreciated.

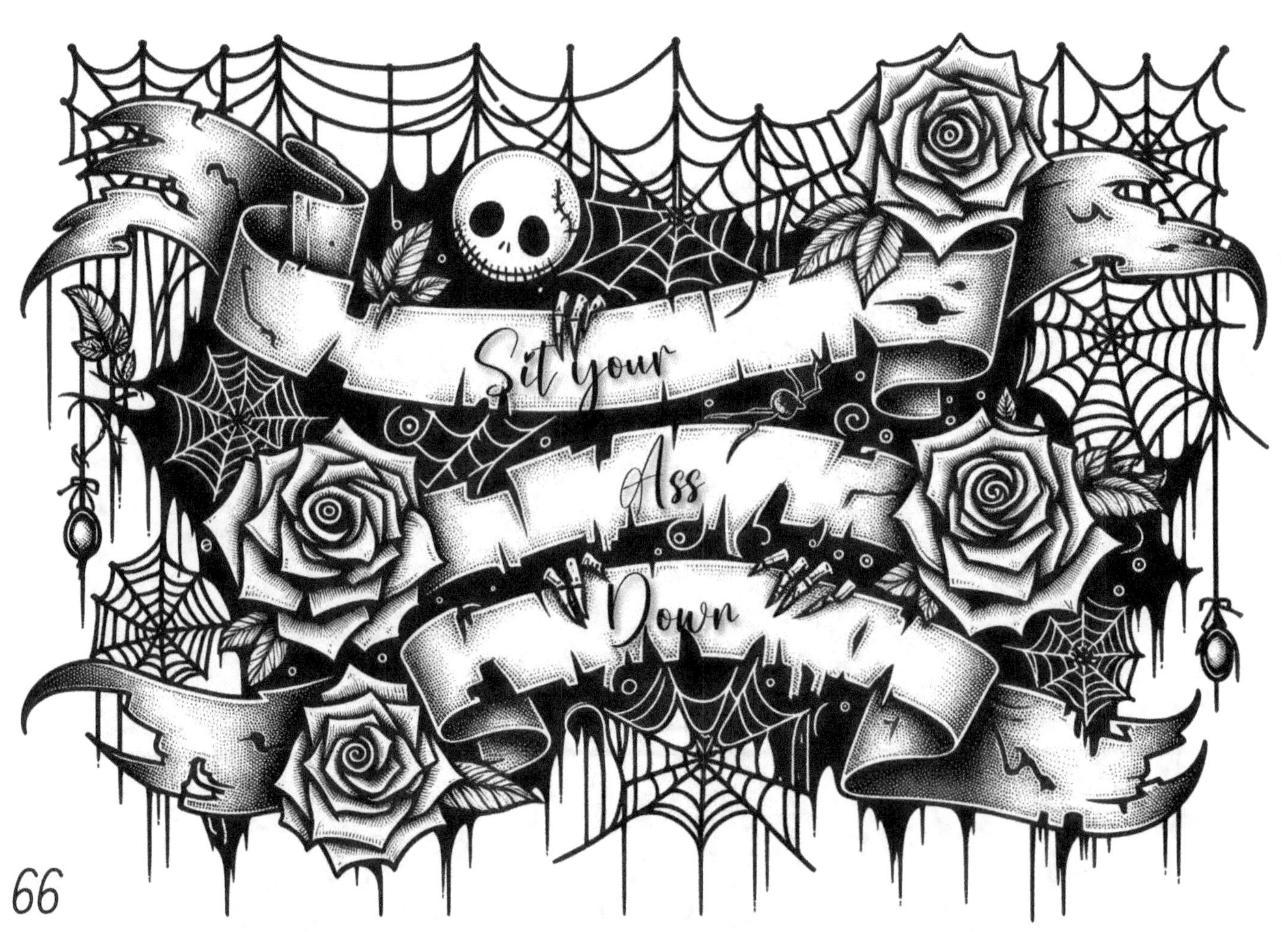

3 The Emoji Emphasis:

For a modern twist, one couple used emojis to convey their cheeky message. Each card featured the guest's name followed by a string of emojis, including the wink, the peace sign, and yes, the middle finger. It was a subtle nod for the tech-savvy crowd and a fun conversation starter.

4 The Personalized Pun:

Drawing inspiration from each guest's personality or profession, one couple created pun-filled place cards like:

The Top-Notch Teacher [Guest's Name]

The Top-Notch Teacher [Guest's Name]

The Kick-Ass Chef
[Guest's Name]

The Kick-Ass Chef
[Guest's Name]

The Brilliantly Badass Banker
[Guest's Name]

The Brilliantly Badass Banker
[Guest's Name]

This personalized touch showed guests that the couple had put thought into each card and added a layer of intimacy to the event.

Tips for Crafting Your Own Pizzazz-Filled Place Card:

Consistency is Key: Ensure that the tone and design of your place cards match the overall theme of your wedding.

Consider the Setting: If you're having a more formal event, opt for subtler humor to avoid clashing with the ambiance.

Personalize Where Possible: Adding personal touches, whether through puns or compliments, can make guests feel valued and included.

Conclusion:

Place cards, while small, can make a big impact on your wedding's atmosphere. By infusing them with humor and personality, you can set a fun and relaxed tone for your event. Whether you choose bold statements or subtle nods,, the key is to stay true to your style and consider your audience. After all, it's all about creating memorable moments for you and your guests.

Introduction:

The wedding menu is more than just a list of dishes; it's an opportunity to showcase the couple's personality and set the tone for the meal. For those looking to make a bold statement, a touch of profanity can transform a traditional menu into a memorable conversation piece. Let's delve into some real-life examples that left guests both hungry and amused.

1. The Bold Header:

One couple decided to kick off their menu with a bang, using the headline:

Get Ready to Eat Some Damn Good Food!

Get Ready to Eat Some Damn Good Food!

The dishes listed below were described in a more traditional manner, but the initial proclamation set a fun and relaxed tone for the meal.

2. The Dish Descriptions:

Another couple took a playful approach to their dish descriptions:

The Salad
That's Fresher Than You

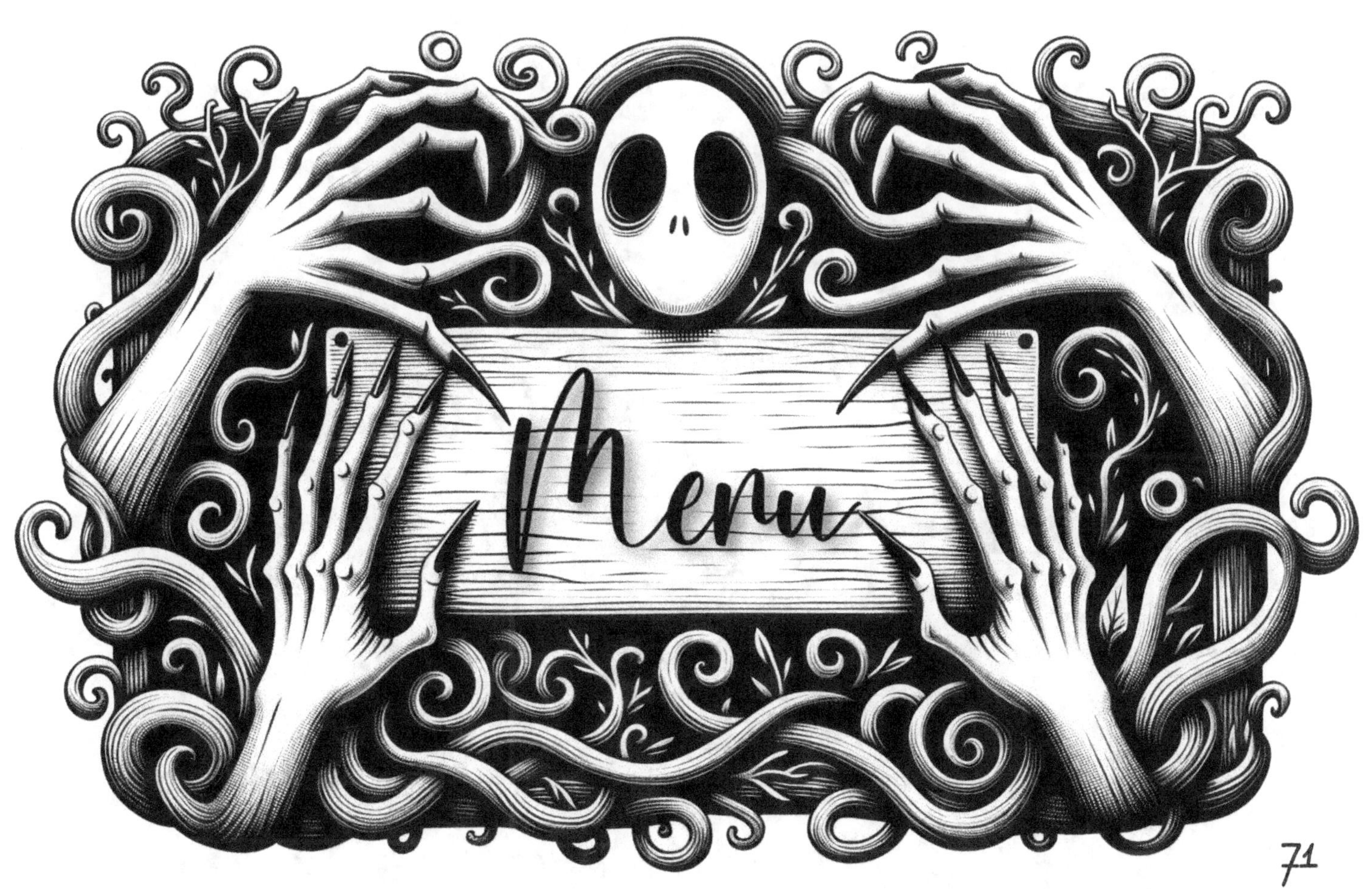

The Steak
That Doesn't Give a Fuck
About Your Diet

The Steak
That Doesn't Give a Fuck
About Your Diet

The Dessert
That'll Make You Say
Holy Shit!

The Dessert That'll Make You Say 'Holy Shit!

These cheeky descriptions added humor and made each dish feel special and enticing.

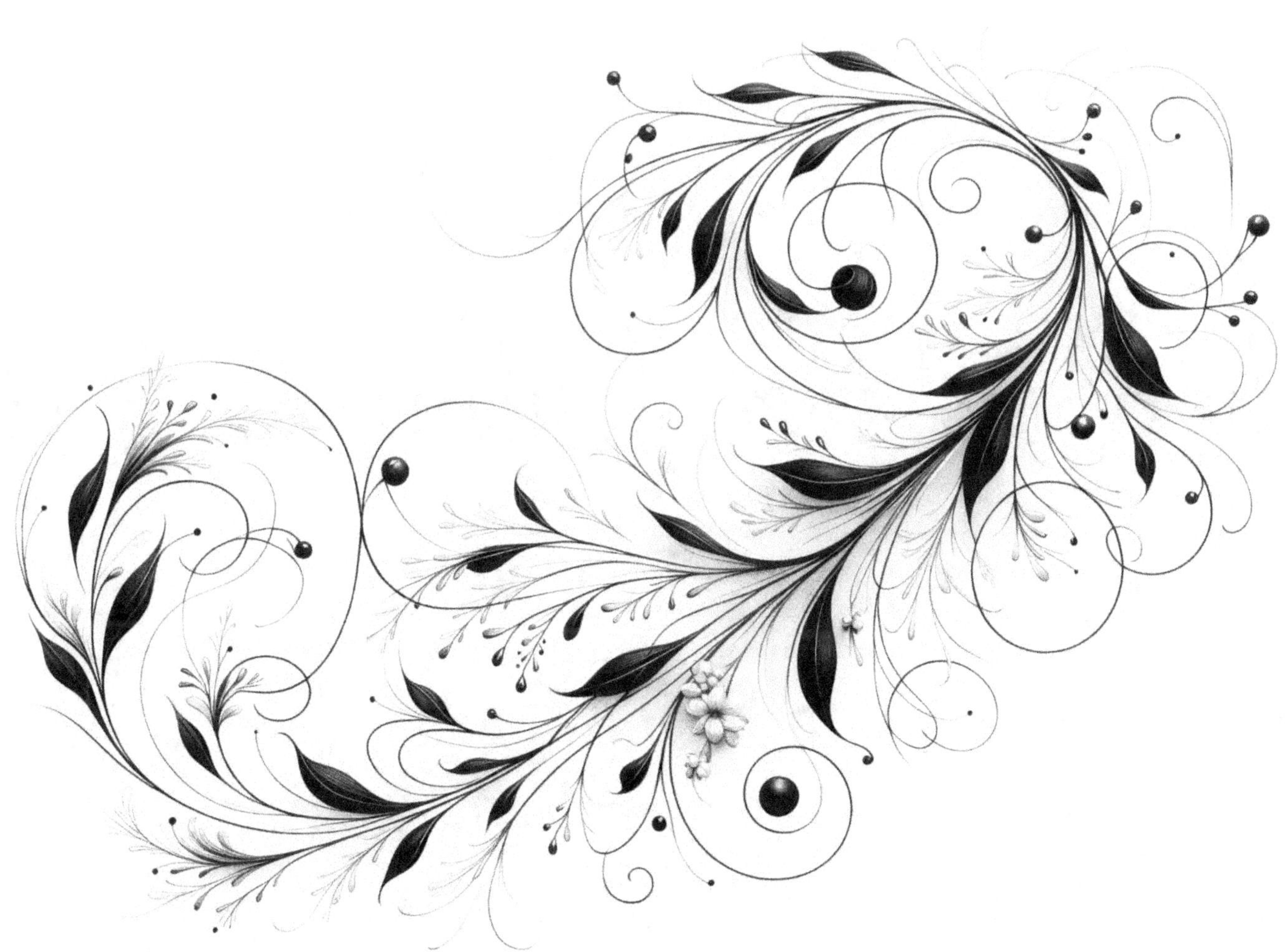

Drinks weren't left out of the fun. One menu featured a section titled "Boozy Beverages for Those Who Like to Party Hard." Options included:

The Tipsy Tequila Tango

The Fucking Fabulous Fizz

The Gobsmacked Gin & Tonic

The Gobsmacked Gin & Tonic

The Gobsmacked Gin & Tonic

4 The Vegetarian Option:

Acknowledging the often-limited options for vegetarians at weddings, one couple humorously titled their vegetarian section:

For Those Who Don't Do Meat (We Got You, Don't Worry)

For Those Who Don't Do Meat (We Got You, Don't Worry)

The dishes listed were equally enticing, ensuring vegetarian guests felt considered and catered for.

One couple shared a brief story of their first date, where they argued over the best type of pizza. Their menu playfully offered both options under the titles:

His Damn Delicious Deep Dish

Her Perfect Thin Crust (The Clear Winner)

This personal touch not only added humor but also gave guests a glimpse into the couple's relationship.

Tips for Crafting Your Statement Menu:

Balance is Essential: While humor is the goal, ensure the menu remains informative. Guests should know what they're eating.

Consider Dietary Restrictions: If offering dishes for specific dietary needs, ensure they're clearly marked and described with the same care and humor as other items.

Quality First: While playful descriptions are fun, the quality of the food should always be the star. Ensure your menu reflects the deliciousness of the dishes.

Conclusion:

A wedding menu with personality can elevate the dining experience and leave a lasting impression on guests. Whether you opt for bold proclamations, cheeky dish descriptions, or personal anecdotes, the key is to be authentic and considerate of your guests' dining experience. After all, a memorable menu is one that combines humor with delectable dishes.

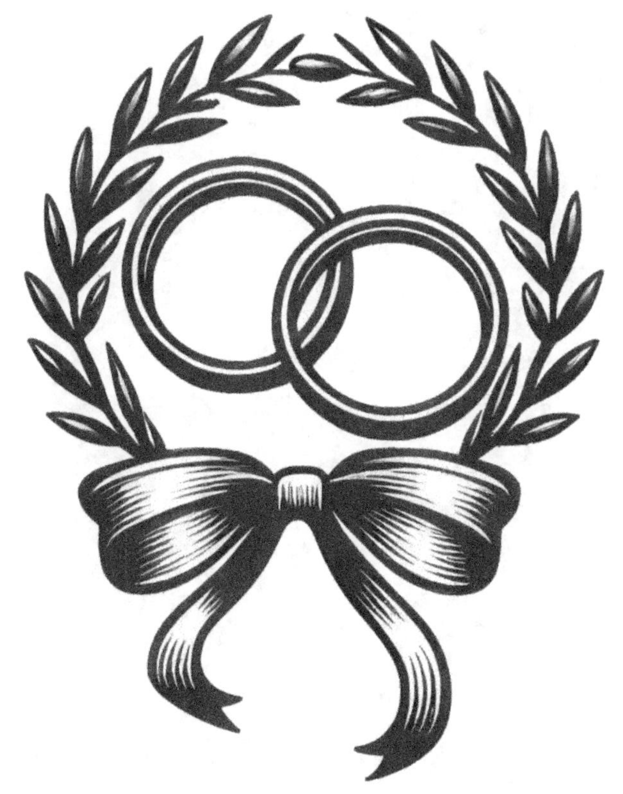

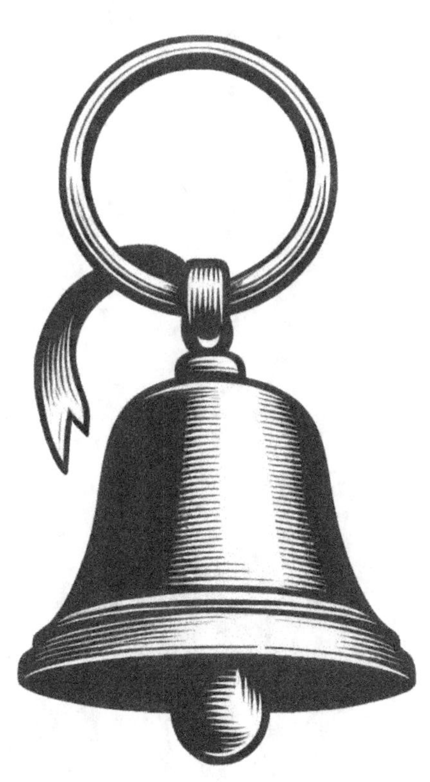

Introduction:

Expressing gratitude is a cherished tradition following a wedding, and thank you cards offer a personal touch in conveying appreciation to guests. For couples who've embraced a cheeky theme throughout their wedding, maintaining that tone in their thank you cards can leave a lasting impression. Let's explore some standout examples that combined gratitude with a touch of audacity.

1. The Straightforward Thanks:

One couple kept it simple yet memorable with their card reading:

Thanks for showing up and getting drunk with us. Best. Day. Ever

This candid approach resonated with guests, capturing the fun spirit of the wedding.

2. The Playful Appreciation:

Another couple opted for a more playful tone, with their card stating:

You're the Fucking Best! Thanks for making our day epic.

You're the Fucking Best! Thanks for making our day epic.

Accompanied by a photo of the couple laughing, it was a heartfelt and humorous gesture.

For a more personalized approach, one couple sent out cards tailored to each guest, referencing specific moments or gifts. For instance:

Thanks for the damn fancy blender. Smoothies on us next time!

This individual touch made each guest feel truly valued.

Drawing inspiration from memorable moments during the wedding, one couple's card read:

Remember when Uncle Bob danced on the table? Thanks for being part of those crazy memories!

Remember when Uncle Bob danced on the table? Thanks for being part of those crazy memories!

Accompanied by candid photos from the wedding, it was a delightful trip down memory lane.

Anticipating future gatherings, one couple's thank you card read:

Thanks for the love, laughter, and that generous gift. Let's do it again soon. Drinks at our place?

Thanks for the love, laughter, and that generous gift. Let's do it again soon. Drinks at our place?

This not only expressed gratitude but also extended an invitation for future fun.

Tips for Crafting Memorable Thank You Cards:

Photos Add a Personal Touch: Including candid or fun photos from the wedding can make your thank you cards even more special.

Quality Matters: Invest in good quality paper and printing. It reflects the care and appreciation you feel towards your guests.

Stay True to Yourselves: While humor is great, ensure it feels authentic to you as a couple. Your genuine gratitude should shine through.

Conclusion:

Thank you cards are a reflection of your appreciation for the love and support of your guests. By infusing them with humor and personality, you can ensure they're not only appreciated but also remembered. Whether you opt for candid messages, personal anecdotes, or playful jokes, the key is to convey your heartfelt thanks in a way that's uniquely you.

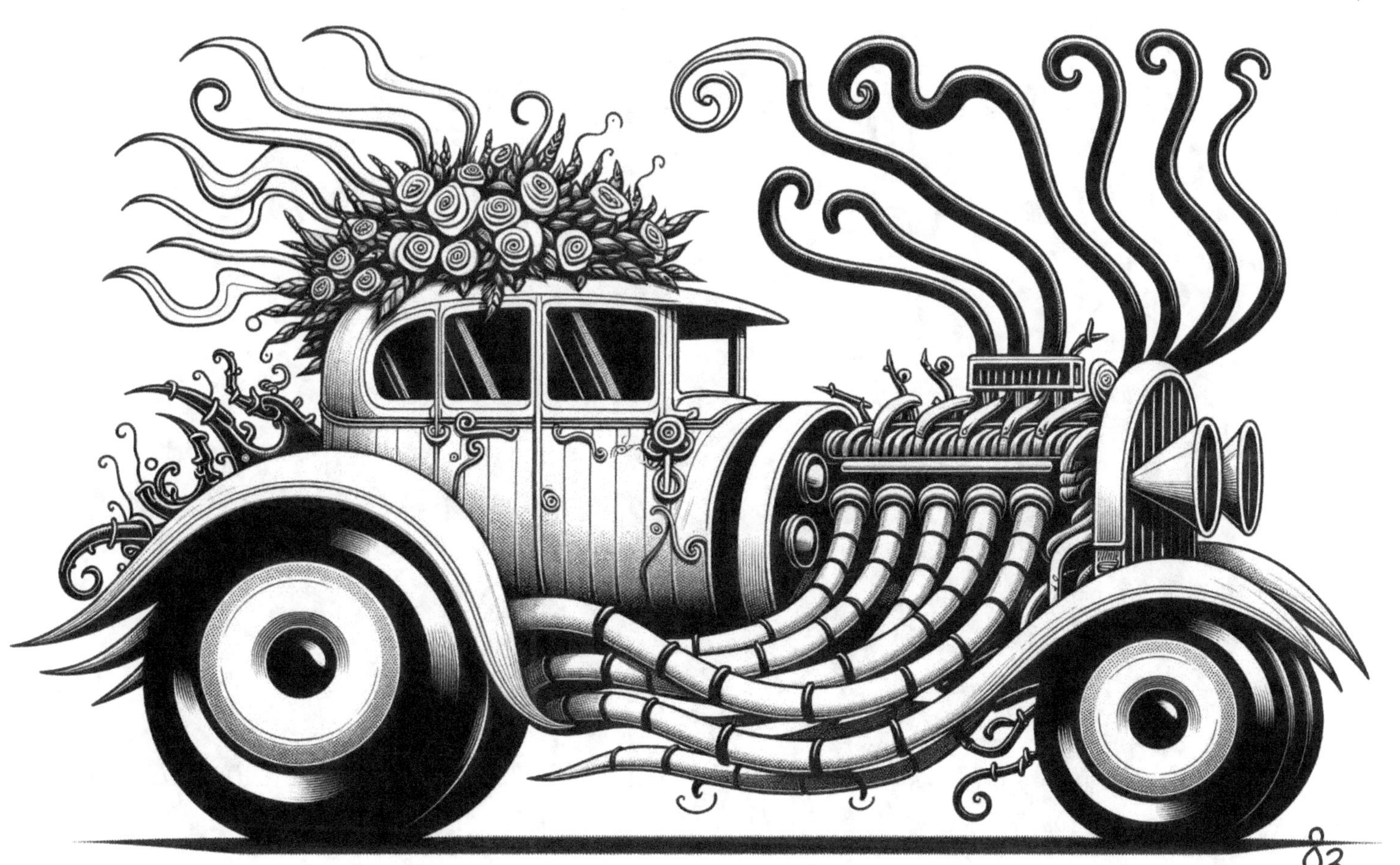

Introduction:

Beyond the mainstays of wedding stationery like invitations, place cards, menus, and thank you cards, there are numerous other pieces that can be infused with a touch of cheeky charm. From programs to save-the-dates, let's delve into some creative examples where couples have incorporated profanity to make their wedding truly stand out.

1. The Unconventional Program:

One couple decided to give their guests a chuckle right from the ceremony's start with a program titled:

Here's How This Shit is Going to Go Down

Here's How This Shit is Going to Go Down

The inside detailed the order of events with equally humorous descriptions, setting a light-hearted tone for the ceremony.

Building anticipation for the big day, a save-the-date card read:

Clear your calendar, and get your party pants ready. Shit's about to get real on [date]

Clear your calendar, and get your party pants ready. Shit's about to get real on [date]

This playful heads-up ensured guests marked their calendars with eagerness.

3. The Cheeky Wedding Website:

Embracing the digital age, one couple's wedding website URL was "www.[Couple's Names)BigFuckingDay.com." The site itself was filled with humorous anecdotes, cheeky FAQs, and playful photos, offering guests a taste of what to expect

4. The Guest Book with a Twist:

Moving away from the traditional guest book, one couple had a sign next to theirs that read:

Leave us a damn good piece

of advice or a joke.

Make it count!

Leave us a damn good piece

of advice or a joke.

Make it count!

This prompted guests to get creative with their messages, resulting in a keepsake filled with laughter and wisdom.

5 The Favors They Won't Forget:

As a parting gift, guests received small bags labeled.

Recovery Kit for Tomorrow's Hangover. You're Welcome.

Recovery Kit for Tomorrow's Hangover. You're Welcome.

Inside were essentials like pain relievers, water, and snacks. It was a humorous nod to the festivities of the night and a thoughtful gesture.

Consistency is Crucial: While each piece can have its unique flair, ensure there's a consistent theme or tone throughout all your wedding stationery.

Function and Form: While humor is a fantastic element, ensure each piece still serves its primary function effectively.

Engage and Involve: Use these pieces as an opportunity to engage your guests, whether it's through interactive elements, prompts, or shared jokes.

Conclusion:

Every element of your wedding, no matter how small, offers an opportunity to showcase your personality as a couple. By infusing humor and a touch of profanity into various pieces of your wedding stationery, you can ensure your big day is not only memorable but also genuinely reflective of your unique style. Whether it's a cheeky program, a playful website, or unforgettable favors, the key is to have fun and let your love shine through.

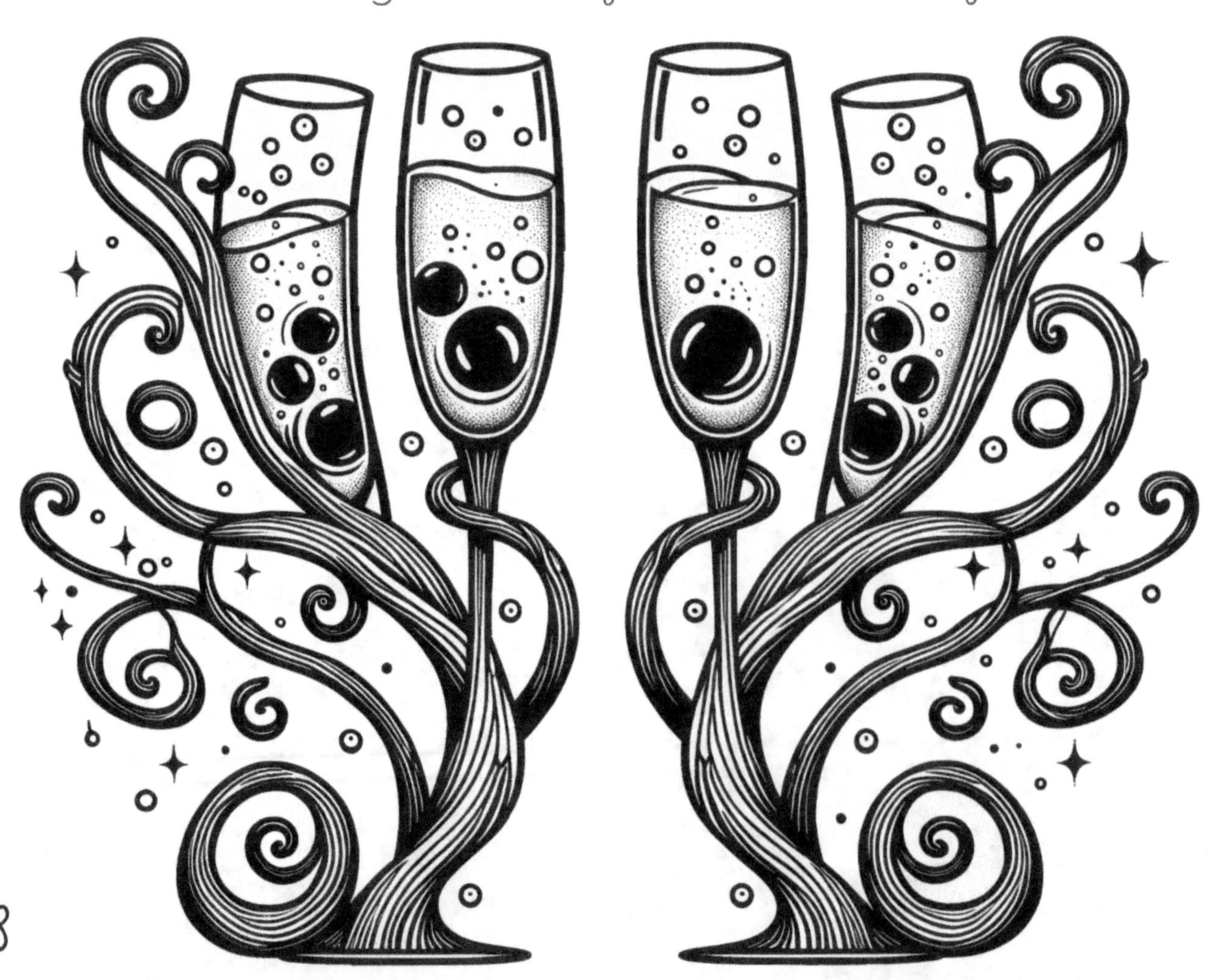

Chapter 7: Embracing the Feedback and Looking Ahead

Introduction:

After the wedding festivities have concluded and the cheeky stationery pieces have made their mark, it's time to reflect on the impact, gather feedback, and look ahead. This chapter delves into the reactions from guests, lessons learned, and how to carry forward this unique style into future events and milestones.

Section 7.1: Guest Reactions: The Good, The Bad, and The Hilarious

1. The Good: Cheers and Chuckles

The Laughing Aunt: At one wedding, an aunt known for her conservative views surprised everyone. After reading her cheeky place card, she burst into laughter, exclaiming, "This is the best damn wedding I've ever been to!"

The Complimentary Cousin: Another couple received feedback from a cousin who said, "Your invitation was the talk of our house for weeks! We've never seen anything like it. Kudos for being so bold and original."

2. The Bad: Raised Eyebrows and Concerns

The Worried Grandparent: One couple recounted how their grandmother expressed concern about the "language" used in the wedding program, gently reminding them that "weddings are a dignified affair."

The Confused Friend: Another guest, unfamiliar with the couple's sense of humor, admitted they initially thought the profane save-the-date was a printing error. They said, "I was about to call you to let you know of the mistake until I realized it was intentional!"

3 The Hilarious: *Unintended Consequences and Moments*

The Misplaced Menu: *At one reception, a cheeky menu ended up at a neighboring event due to a mix-up. The other party's reaction? They sent over a bottle of champagne with a note: "Thanks for the laugh! Best menu we've ever seen."*

The Viral Invitation: *One couple's unique invitation became an internet sensation. After a guest shared it online, it went viral, leading to comments like, "Where's my invite?" and "Wedding goals right here!"*

Tips for Navigating Varied Reactions:

Know Your Audience: *While it's your special day, consider the sensibilities of your guests. It's essential to strike a balance between personal expression and respect for attendees.*

Open Communication: *If you anticipate strong reactions, consider giving close family members a heads-up. This can help manage expectations and ensure no one is caught off guard.*

Embrace the Feedback: *Whether it's praise or critique, take it in stride. Every reaction is a testament to the uniqueness of your wedding.*

Conclusion:

Guest reactions are a testament to the impact of your wedding choices. While not every response will be positive, the goal is to create a memorable experience that reflects you as a couple. Embrace the good, learn from the bad, and always cherish the hilarious moments that make your wedding truly unforgettable.

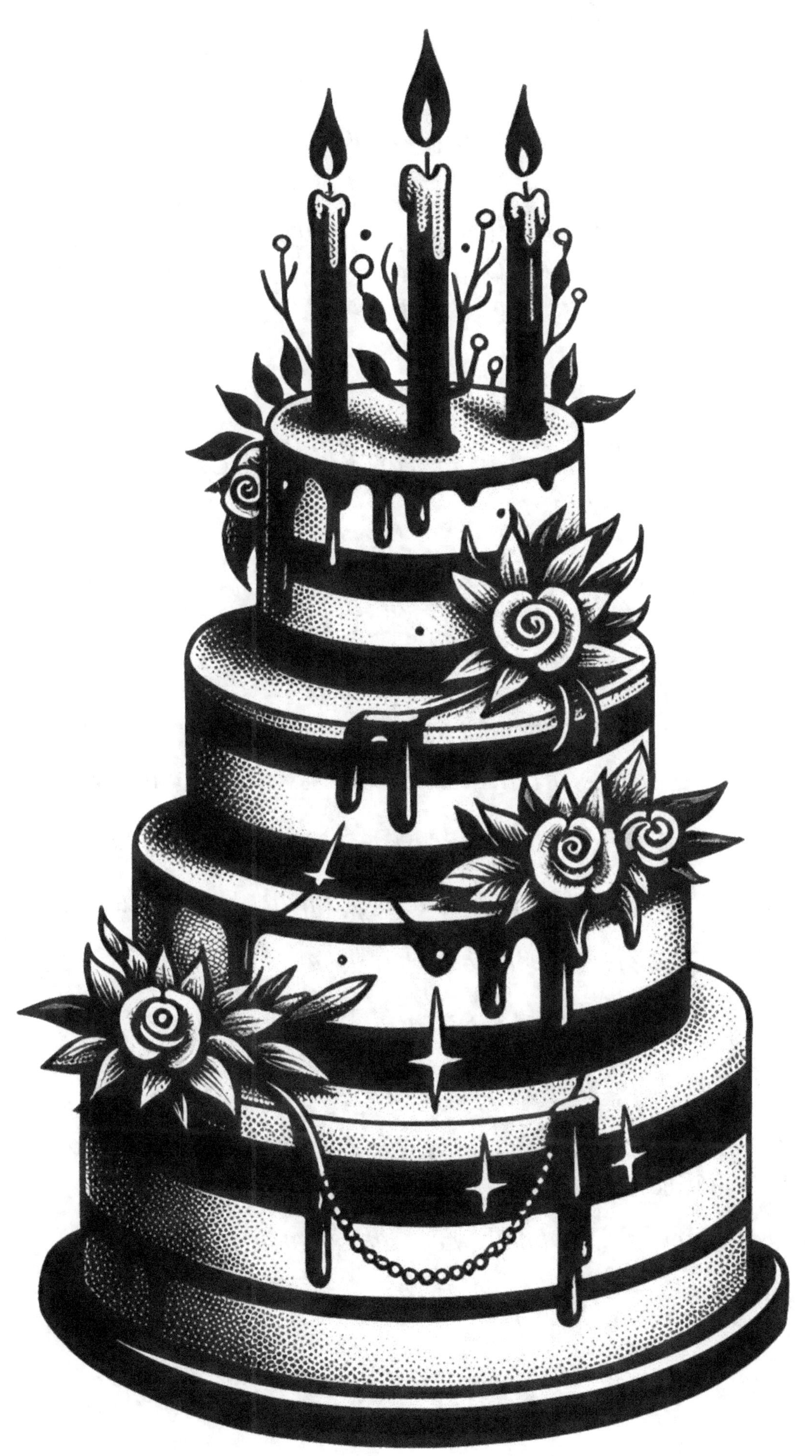

Introduction:

Swear words, often considered taboo in polite conversation, have a rich history and can provide insight into cultural norms, taboos, and linguistic evolution. This glossary provides a list of popular swear words from various English-speaking regions, along with their meanings.

American Swear Words (US):

Fuck: One of the most widely recognized swear words. Originated from Fornication Under the Consent of the King. Often used to express frustration or surprise.

Fuck you: A direct offense towards someone, expressing anger or disdain.

Shit: Refers to feces but is often used to express disappointment or surprise.

Piss off: A way to tell someone to leave or express annoyance.

Dick head: Used to describe someone acting unfairly or unjustly.

Asshole: Refers to a part of the body but is also used as an insult.

Son of a bitch: Used to express frustration or surprise.

Bastard: Refers to an illegitimate child. Used as an insult.

Bitch: A term that can be derogatory when directed towards someone but can also be used casually.

Damn: An expression of disappointment or surprise.

Cunt: A very offensive term, especially towards women.

British Swear Words (UK):

Bollocks: Refers to testicles but is also used to express disappointment.

Bugger: Used to show annoyance or surprise.

Bloody Hell: An exclamation of surprise or frustration.

Choad: Another term for penis.

Crikey: Used to show astonishment.

Rubbish: Refers to trash or something of poor quality.

Shag: Means to have sex.

Wanker: Refers to a person who masturbates.

Taking the piss: Means someone is not being serious or is wasting time.

Twat: A derogatory term, similar to 'pussy'.

Australian Swear Words (AU):

Bloody Oath: An exclamation of agreement or support.

Root: Similar to the British 'shag', means to have sex.

Get Stuffed: A way to tell someone to leave or that you disagree with them.

Bugger me: An expression of surprise.

Fair suck of the sav: Asking for a fair chance or opportunity.

The use of swear words can be offensive and is often culturally and contextually dependent. It's essential to exercise caution and be aware of the potential impact on listeners.

Appendix B: Calligraphy Styles and Their Origins

Introduction:

Calligraphy, the art of beautiful handwriting, has a rich and diverse history spanning different cultures and eras. This appendix delves into various calligraphy styles, their unique characteristics, and their historical origins, providing readers with a deeper appreciation of this elegant art form.

Gothic Script:

Origin: Originating in Medieval Europe, Gothic script gained immense popularity between the 12th and 15th centuries. It was a time when cathedrals with Gothic architecture were on the rise, and this script became a hallmark of the era.

Characteristics: Gothic script is dense, angular, and has a somewhat intimidating appearance. The letters are uniform and narrow, making the text appear compact. Its ornate capitals are a standout feature, often adorned with intricate designs. Due to its solemn and formal appearance, it was the preferred choice for religious texts, official documents, and manuscripts.

Italic Script:

Origin: Born during the Renaissance period in Italy, Italic script emerged in the 15th century as artists and writers sought a more fluid and elegant way of writing.

Characteristics: Italic script is characterized by its slanted, flowing letters. Unlike the dense Gothic, Italic is more rounded and open, making it highly readable. Its elegance made it popular for personal correspondence and literature.

Copperplate:

Origin: Copperplate script traces its roots back to 18th-century England. It was named after the copper plates on which it was engraved for printing.

Characteristics: The script is known for its contrasting strokes: thick downward strokes paired with delicate upward ones. Written with a pointed nib, Copperplate exudes formality and refinement, making it a favorite for invitations and official documents.

Kufic Script:

Origin: Developed between the 7th and 10th centuries, Kufic is the oldest form of Arabic calligraphy. It emerged in early Islamic regions and became the standard for writing the Quran for several centuries.

Characteristics: Kufic is geometric, angular, and often appears block-like. Its strict patterns and shapes made it ideal for architectural inscriptions, especially on mosques and monuments.

Cursive Script:

Origin: Cursive script was developed in Western Europe as writers sought a faster way to pen down their thoughts without compromising on beauty.

Characteristics: As the name suggests, cursive script flows seamlessly, with letters often connected in a continuous manner. It's designed for speed, efficiency, and legibility, making it a common choice for everyday writing.

Brush Script:

Origin: Brush script has its roots in East Asia, particularly in countries like China and Japan, where the art of brush painting and writing has been practiced for centuries.

Characteristics: Unlike other scripts that use a nib, brush script is crafted with a brush. This gives it a fluid, expressive style, with each stroke reflecting the artist's emotions, intentions, and mastery over the brush.

Uncial Script:

Origin: Uncial script was prevalent in early Christian writings, spanning from the 3rd to the 8th centuries. It was a script of choice for many religious manuscripts during this period.

Characteristics: Uncial letters are rounded yet hold a slight angularity. The script exudes a sense of majesty and reverence, making it a fitting choice for religious texts and scriptures.

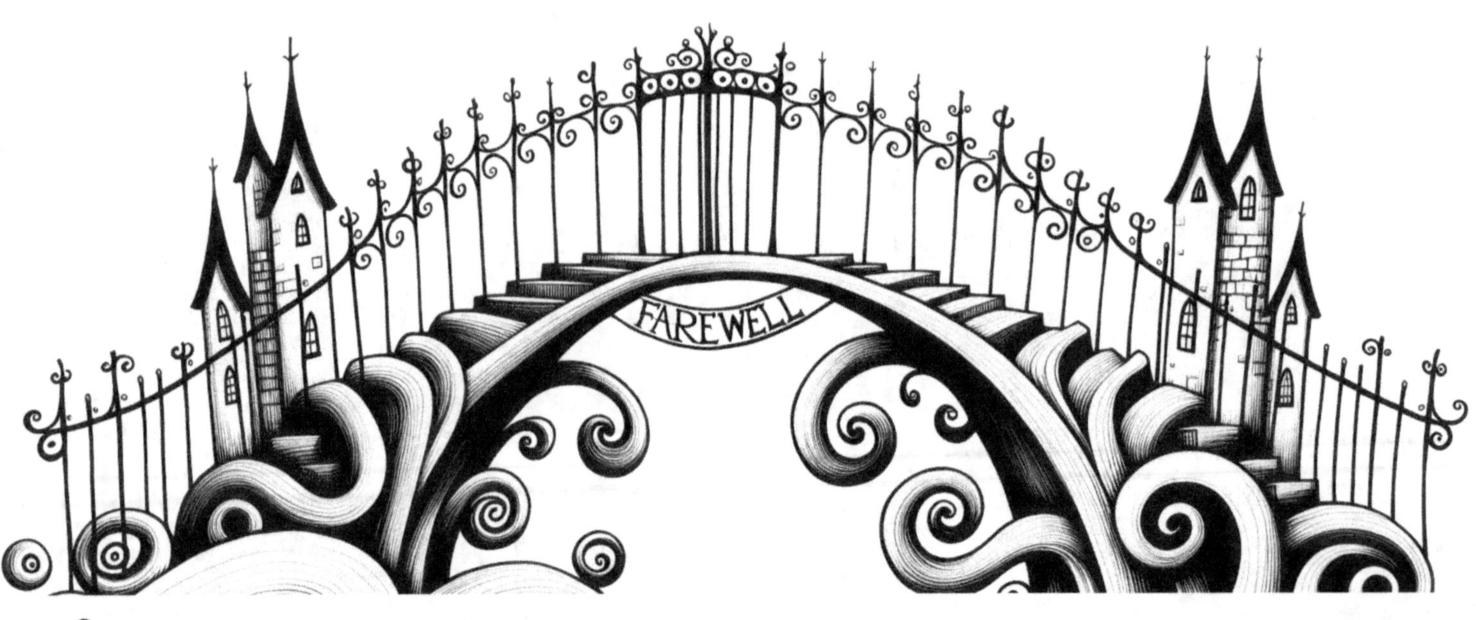

Summary of "The Fucking Wedding Calligraphy Workbook":

"The Fucking Wedding Calligraphy Workbook" is a unique guide to the art of calligraphy, blending traditional lettering techniques with a modern, audacious approach to wedding invitations and decor. This manual offers readers not just the skills to write beautifully but also infuses a touch of humor and rebellion into conventional wedding elements.

Starting with the basics of calligraphy, the workbook introduces readers to the world of profanities and their elegant application in wedding invitations, menus, thank-you cards, and other matrimonial pieces. Each chapter focuses on a specific facet of wedding calligraphy, providing practical advice, examples, and exercises.

Beyond traditional calligraphy techniques, the book also offers a contemporary design perspective, emphasizing individuality and authenticity. The appendices provide practical resources such as a swear word glossary, censored calligraphy templates, and a guide to various calligraphic styles.

In essence, "The Fucking Wedding Calligraphy Workbook" is the perfect guide for modern couples looking to add a personal touch to their wedding while having fun and learning the art of calligraphy.

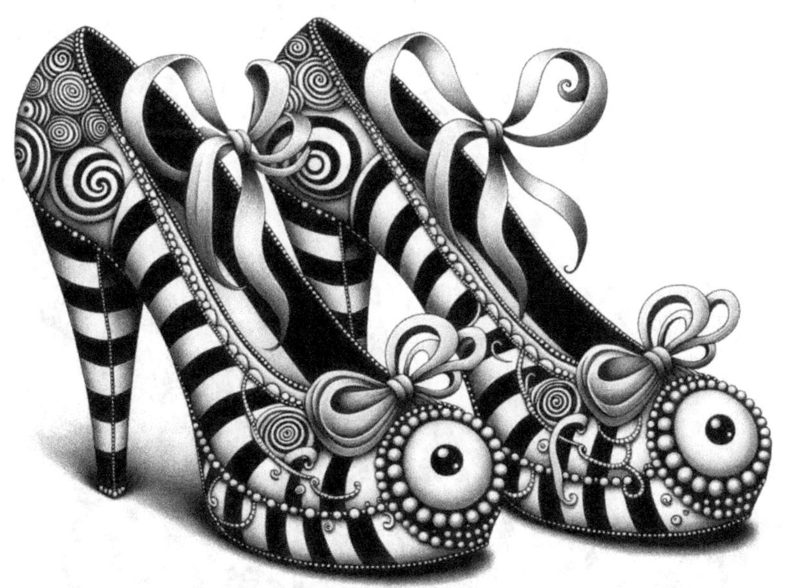

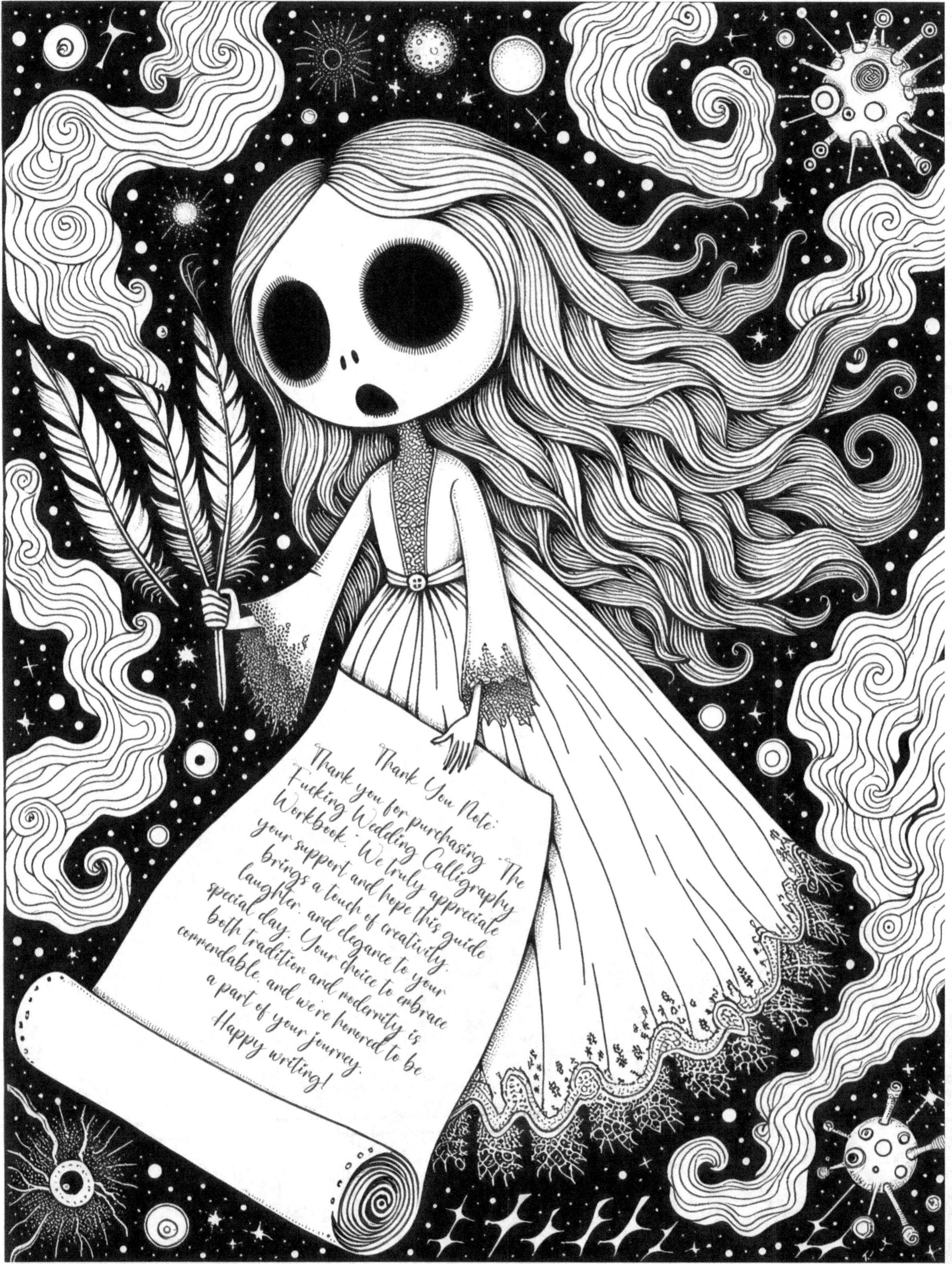

Thank You Note:
Thank you for purchasing "The Fucking Wedding Calligraphy Workbook." We truly appreciate your support and hope this guide brings a touch of creativity, laughter, and elegance to your special day. Your choice to embrace both tradition and modernity is commendable, and we're honored to be a part of your journey.
Happy writing!

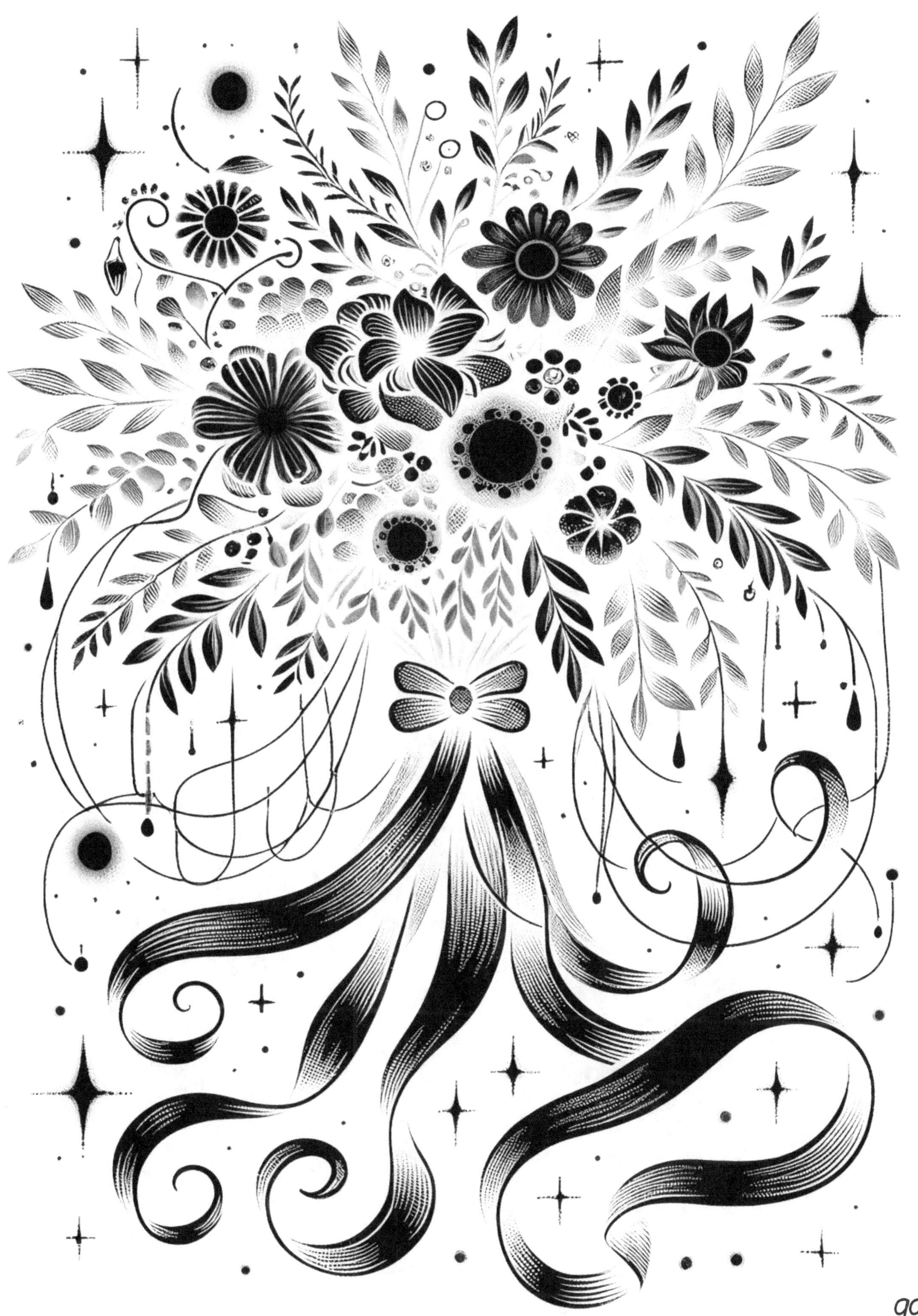

99